The Testimonies of the Sons of Israel
& the Message of the Plates of Brass

by Reed R. Simonsen

Supplemental to The Gospel Feast Series
Book C

"Who's on the Lord's Side? You!"
Chose a side dish and Feast On!"

Thank Yous!

To my parents, whose faithful examples of raising a family in a Mormon home has served as examples for many. I have often reflected on how I, like Joseph of Egypt was raised by parents worthy to bear the good name of a Holy God. They are as Rachel and Jacob to me, and I am grateful.

I have many people to thank, a few are yet living, most have passed beyond: Joseph Smith, Jr., Fred Jepson, John Heinerman, Jim Jepson, Peter Simonsen, David Sexton and Conrad Denke and of course my parents, who have always encouraged my flights of obsessive research, digging-and-digging into history until answers are found. Thank you!

A Note to the Reader: I am occasionally asked, "So, who are these books written for? Sometimes it seems you are writing to Latter-day Saints and sometimes it seems you are writing for Christians-at-Large and sometimes it seems like you don't know." The answer is yes. Enjoy the book.

In order to simplify confusion the following terms mean:

> Mormon: The Church of Jesus Christ of Latter-day Saints.
>
> Mormondom: The culture of Mormonism.
>
> Mormonism: The doctrine, beliefs, and worldview of the Latter-day Saints held either officially or unofficially.
>
> Saints: Members of The Church of Jesus Christ of Latter-day Saints.
>
> Latter-day Saints: Members of The Church of Jesus Christ of Latter-day Saints.
>
> Secular-Christianity: Christian philosophies and organizations which are traditionally held but are wrong.
>
> Restored Church: The Church of Jesus Christ of Latter-day Saints.
>
> B.C.E.: Before the Christian Era. (the same as B.C.)
>
> C.E.: In the Christian Era (the same as A.D.)

Nothing in this work is meant to offend anyone, unless of course you're easily offended, and if you are easily offended, get over yourself   the whole world isn't just about you. See the chapter on arrogant Simeon and how God can help you get over yourself. The vast majority of scriptural quotes are from the *King James Version* with some translational clarifications for modernity. The opinions expressed herein are the opinions of their respective authors.

This is supplemental Volume C in Reed Simonsen's *Gospel Feast Series*. Release v1i. *(cs8203851)*

Vol. 1: *Daniel & the Last Days;* Vol. 2: *Jonah;* Vol. 3: *Ruth;* Vol. 4: *Zechariah;* Vol. 5: *Ezekiel;* Vol. 6: *Revelation;*, and Vols. 7-9: *Genesis* are also available in hard copy. Some volumes are also available as eBooks for use on Apple iProducts from Apple's online iBookstore or in ePub format for Kindle and Nook from Amazon. The entire series is available at www.GospelFeastBooks.com.

Table of Contents

Illustrations

Apologies to all the artists herein for differing reasons. I have chosen art in this volume for its emotional value, hence the intended subject matter is not necessary relevant to the historical nature of the chapter. Therefore, not all illustrations are captioned to avoid confusion.

Cover Art: based on Jacob et l'angle by Gustave Moreau and Detail of Death of Mother Rachel at Bethlehem by Gustav Ferdinand Metz, circa 1847.

pg. 42: Judah Propositions to Tamar by Emile Vernet, 1840.

pg. 80: Detail of The Remorse of Orestes by William Bouguereau, 1862.

pg. 97: The red deer (Cervus elaphus) is one of the largest deer species.

pg. 111: Death of Mother Rachel by Gustav Ferdinand Metz, c. 1847

pg. 129: The Grain Distribution Center at Saqqara Egypt build by Father Joseph the vice-pharaoh.

pg. 130: Joseph Reunited with His Brothers (especially Benjamin whom he's hugging) by Léon Pierre Urbain Bourgeois, oil on canvas, at the Musée Municipal Frédéric Blandin, Nevers, 1863.

pg. 140: Jacob Blessing Ephraim and Manasseh by Benjamin West.

pg. 169: The Simonsens. Left: Charlottie Merrill Simonsen. Right: Brigham City Mayor and Architect, Nels Christian "Chris" Simonsen.

pg. 175: Jacob Hamblin b. April 6th 1819 - d. August 31st 1886. Called the special apostle to the Lamanites and friend of the Native Peoples of the Americas.

pg. 176: Detail of Jacob's Vision of the Ladder Up to Heaven by Jacques Reattu, 1792.

A Book for Now

Woe unto the Children of men for Satan walks among you.
— the Angel of the Presence

You hold in your hands a treasure. A book that I wish I had read in my youth, but one that I am grateful to have read in adulthood. One of Satan's goals, before the return of Jesus Christ, is to destroy gender in the family of God. He will not be entirely successful but there will be much suffering along the way. Suffering that can be avoided.

Gender is the pinnacle of our creation. It was our first choice in the mansions of heaven and is the very purpose of our lives going forward forever. We were made in the very image of the gods, male and female, from the start, and we will be judged male or female and raised male or female in the resurrection. The entire reigning creation of the Father functions on the principle of gender. It is not possible to achieve the founding desires of our hears nor embrace the fullness of Eternal Lives without fulfilling (even in a small degree) a Celestial measure of our creation in the here and now.

This book's treasure lies in its blunt and unabashed commentary on the struggles of masculinity in a fallen world. I am aware of no other book quite like it.

The sons of Father Israel were princes, gods in embryo, men of the church who were well taught but constantly in Lucifer's crosshairs. Demons had marked them for destruction because God had called them to His covenant and blessed them with the priesthood of their grandfather Melchizedek. They were sixth generation Saints, the sons of pioneer ancestors who fought their trials and won their crowns. They had the scriptures of their fathers (Adam, Enoch, Noah, Shem, Abraham, and Isaac). They were given patriarchal blessings and knew the name of their God. Does any of this sound familiar?

In these boys would be typified the signs of the Lord's honor: In Reuben, the glory of a first born heir, who would be called sin for the sake of his brother's advancement; In Dan, the judge of all the world; In Judah, the majesty of a strong and mighty king; but most of all, in Joseph the humble ministering servant of salvation. Biblical scholars have noted over 500 ways in which Joseph's life foreshadowed the Lord's.

These were the chosen family and yet they struggled. They conquered in the end and yet they were sinners. They were men's men who fought envy, anger, pornography, betrayal and the lusts of their heart, and in the end, it will be their names that would adorn the breastplate of the High Priest. Their combined names would make up one of the names of God. Their same names will yet adorn the gates of Lady Zion when the Lord God comes to rule and reign. Each of us will yet bare one of their names as our inheritance in the greatest gift of God.

Their testimonies are a treasure. Men need their candid guidance in our world of gender confusion and women need their deeper insights into the struggles of their fathers, sons and husbands. Modern sons of God often judge themselves by ridiculously high standards and God's daughters expect their men to be perfect *the day they take them off the shelf.* We forget that this is the day of our trial. We will get there but not right out of the box. These attitudes are unrealistic and are thereby cannon fodder for Lucifer in his attacks against us.

THE BRASS PLATES OF LABAN

So why the title of this book? *Book of Mormon* readers know the story of the *Brass Plates*. It is one of the most shocking stories we have in our scriptural canon. It still elicits controversy when it is taught in Sunday School. It is a difficult read for the harsh reality that it implies. It certainly affected Nephi deeply; so much so, that years after the event, he still wrote out a justification for how he obtained it and why. To be called upon to behead a man, at the tender age of 16! I can't imagine it. What a price to pay for the word of God! These plates must have been very special, priceless even. So just what were they? Let's recount the background briefly before moving on.

Prior to the fall of Jerusalem by Nebuchadnezzar, a wealthy man, and prophet, named Lehi had a dream. Many prophets in the land were having dreams and many were warning Judea that God was nearly done putting up with their wickedness. The ten northern tribes had long since been taken away into captivity, and soon the same fate would fall upon the Kingdom of Judah if they did not speedily repent. They did not, and various prophets, righteous patriarchs, and basically anyone who would listen, were fleeing the land before the Babylonian Army arrived to take them away. Lehi's dream warned him to take his family and some friends and live out in the vast desert of Arabia while the Lord prepared to take them to a promised land far from the dangers of Babylon.

It was while Lehi's family was out in the wilderness that he received the command to send his sons back to Jerusalem and get their hands on a set of scriptures which they called *The Plates of Brass* or the *Brass Plates*. Many Mormons read this story and say, "Sure, you know the Brass Plates – the scriptures – it's important to have the scriptures with you." And it ends there.

Now of course it is important to have the scriptures with you, but Gospel Feasters know that we do not take things for granted in a Gospel Feast. We pray and ponder, push and prod, study the text and hold fast to the good we find while looking for more. We are feasters! We cannot just brush by the *Brass Plates* so easily. We have questions and lots of them. So, we ask the questions and listen to the spirit. We take a few keys and open doors. We knock and listen and feast!

Here is the first question: Why didn't Lehi, a prophet, have a copy of the scriptures? Does that make any sense? Every synagogue and home in Israel was required to read from the *Torah* and study the *Books of Moses* continually. That was the law. A righteous father was REQUIRED to read and study the law with his children. It was not optional. Lehi HAD TO HAVE HAD the scriptures. If Israelites were anything, they were a literate people. They spoke, wrote, and could read Hebrew. Further we know that Lehi, (as with many of the tribe of Joseph) also knew Egyptian; a legacy from their Pharaoh-fathers. So, how is it possible that a prominent prophet didn't have the scriptures? We have asked the question. Asking the right question will lead to the right answer. And, we are already upon it.

Lehi did have the scriptures. He had the *Torah* which we know is the marriage contract between Jehovah and Israel. That is the first five books of the *Bible* that we have today: *Genesis, Exodus, Leviticus, Numbers & Deuteronomy;* I also now believe that it included a sixth book — *Jubilees.* These books belonged to all the people by contractual right and were the books from which church readings and talks were given at synagogues and from which parents taught their children literacy at home. These were not the *Brass Plates.* So what were the *Brass Plates?*

The answer is going to amaze and delight you! Do you want to read some of what is on the Brass Plates right now? If you are willing to exercise a little faith, try and test the Spirit, then take a little journey with me?

Turn the page....

I promise to answer your next question when you get to chapter 13, but for now, enjoy the journey, listen to the Spirit and see what the still, small voice says to your heart.

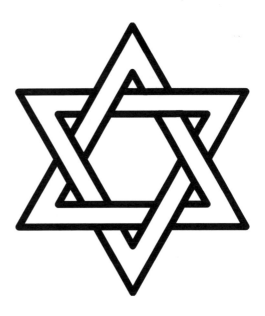

Chapter One

Reuben

*And now hear me, my children, what things I saw concerning the seven
spirits of deceit, when I repented. — Reuben*

Reuben was the first-born son of Jacob and Leah. His
mother named him "Seen Son" meaning God has seen that I
needed a son." Much of Leah's hope for being a beloved wife
came from her desire to give Jacob a family, something that
Rachel was unable to do. The Lord's exact purposes in all of this
is not clear, except that it appears by allowing these sisters to vie
in competition over family, Jacob would end up with 12 sons and
a daughter. Considering that Abraham and Sarah had one son
and Isaac and Rebekah had twin boys, large families were not the
norm for the chosen house. Jacobs many young boys were all
born in a relatively short amount of time and did give him a lot
of grief until their mature years, when they grew up and became
the men of God, that God needed them to be. One of the
greatest gifts found in the Testimony of the Patriarchs is the
realization that despite the sins and stupidity of youth, all of the
Sons of Israel turned out to be men worthy of emulation. They
would indeed become in time, the pillars of their father's house
and in our case the very pillars of the holy city we will yet inherit.

In Israel much was expected of an eldest son. By all
accounts, other than allowing himself to be talked into things by
his younger brothers, Reuben tried to be a credit to his family. As
we will discover, the two life choices which haunted him till the
end was his inability to save Joseph from his other brothers and
his bad judgement one night in a fit of drunken passion. It

should stand as a powerful lesson. One can make terrible choices in an instant and then take a lifetime to regret them.

Reuben 1:1 The copy of the Testament of Reuben, even the commands which he gave his sons before he died in the hundred and twenty-fifth year of his life.

2 Two years after the death of Joseph his brother, when Reuben fell ill, his sons and his sons' sons were gathered together to visit him.

3 And he said to them: My children, behold I am dying, and go the way of my fathers.

4 And seeing there Judah, and Gad, and Asher, his brethren, he said to them: Raise me up that I may tell to my brethren and to my children what things I have hidden in my heart, for behold now at length I am passing away.

5 And he arose and kissed them, and said unto them: Hear, my brethren, and do ye my children, give ear to Reuben your father, in the commands which I give unto you.

6 And behold I call to witness against you this day the God of heaven, that ye walk not in the sins of youth and fornication, wherein I was poured out, and defiled the bed of my father Jacob.

7 And I tell you that God smote me with a sore plague in my loins for seven months; and had not my father Jacob prayed for me to the Lord, the Lord would have destroyed me.

8 For I was thirty years old when I wrought the evil thing before the Lord, and for seven months I was sick unto death.

The *Book of Jubilees* records the sad event:

Jubillees 33:2 And Reuben saw Bilhah, Rachel's maid, the concubine of his father, bathing in water in a secret place, and he lusted after her.

3 And he hid himself, and he entered the house of Bilhah at night, and he found her sleeping alone on a bed in her house.

4 And he lay with her *in the dark*, and she awoke and thinking he was Jacob, uncovered the border of her covering and seized him, and cried out in pleasure, and saw, and behold Reuben was lying with her in the bed!

5 And she was ashamed because of him, and released her hand from him, and he fled.

6 And she lamented because of this thing exceedingly, and did not tell it to any one at that time.

7 And when Jacob returned and sought her [for he had been away seeing his father], she said unto him: "I am not clean for thee, for I have been defiled as regards thee; for Reuben hath defiled me, and hath lain with me in the night, and I was asleep, and did not discover until he uncovered my skirt and slept with me." [1]

8 And Jacob was exceedingly wroth with Reuben because he had lain with Bilhah, because he had uncovered his father's skirt.

Since a man and wife are one flesh in the eyes of heaven, Jacob is saying that Reuben had also defiled him, as well as Bilhah. They had both been raped in other words.

9 And Jacob did not approach her again because Reuben had defiled her. And as for any man who uncovereth his father's skirt his deed is wicked exceedingly, for he is abominable before the Lord.

We know from other sources that part of the problems in Jacob's family stemmed from his lingering disgust over having been forced to marry Leah in order to get Rachel. However, since Jacob had agreed to the arrangement in the end, the Lord expected him to be honorable about it all. By all accounts he tried but the scriptures do tell us that Leah often felt like the third wheel. This competition for affection did work its way into Jacob's sons. His older boys all came from Leah and knew that they were the legal heirs in the family. They frequently treated the son's of the mother's maids, Bilhah and Zilphah's, like servants. Leah's sons were unchallenged in their feelings until Joseph was born. The Lord was not okay with this. Further, Reuben as the first son also came to see his father's "handmaids" as his inheritable property, which they were not. He would have been required to provide for them at his father's death, but they were not his *property to enjoy*. Reuben would in the end see the error of his ways and make it right. Here are his own words:

Reuben 1:9 And after this I repented with set purpose of my soul for seven years before the Lord.

10 And wine and strong drink I drank not, and flesh entered not into my mouth, and I ate no pleasant food; but I mourned over my sin, for it was great, such as had not been in Israel.

This is serious repentance; no wine, no meat, no celebratory food for seven years! Reuben would then tell his children that in the pains of his repentance he came to understand that there were seven demons which set out to destroy humanity. This may very well be the origin of the famous *Seven Deadly Sins.*

Reuben 1:11 And now hear me, my children, what things I saw concerning the seven spirits of deceit, when I repented.

12 Seven spirits therefore are appointed against man, and they are the leaders in the works of youth.

In other words, young people are stupid sometimes.

13 And seven other spirits are given to him at his creation, that through them should be done every work of man. Let us speak of these first:

14 The first is the spirit of life, with which the constitution of man is created.

15 The second is the sense of sight, with which ariseth desire.

16 The third is the sense of hearing, with which cometh teaching.

The Jews still teach this. Sin comes from the lust of the eyes, but the Lord whispers to the ears in a still, small, voice.[2]

17 The fourth is the sense of smell, with which tastes are given to draw air and breath.

18 The fifth is the power of speech, with which cometh knowledge.

19 The sixth is the sense of taste, with which cometh the eating of meats and drinks; and by it strength is produced, for in food is the foundation of strength.

20 The seventh is the power of procreation and sexual intercourse, with which through love of pleasure sins enter in.

21 Wherefore it is the last in order of creation, and the first in that of youth, because it is filled with ignorance, and leadeth the youth as a blind man to a pit, and as a beast to a precipice.

22 Besides all these there is an eighth spirit of sleep, with which is brought about the trance of nature and of death.

23 With these spirits are mingled the spirits of error. These are:

24 First, the spirit of fornication is seated in the nature and in the senses;

25 The second, the spirit of insatiableness in the belly;

26 The third, the spirit of fighting, in the liver and gall.

27 The fourth is the spirit of deception and chicanery, that through hyper-aggression and zeal one may seem fair and passionate.

28 The fifth is the spirit of pride, that one may be boastful and arrogant.

29 The sixth is the spirit of lying, in perdition and jealousy to practise deceits, and concealments from kindred and friends.

30 The seventh is the spirit of injustice, with which are thefts and acts of rapacity, that a man may fulfil the desire of his heart; for injustice worketh together with the other spirits by the taking of gifts.

31 And with all these the spirit of sleep is joined which is that of error and fantasy.[3]

32 And so perisheth every young man, darkening his mind from the truth, and not understanding the law of God, nor obeying the admonitions of his fathers, as befell me also in my youth.

33 And now, my children, love the truth, and it will preserve you: hear ye the words of Reuben your father.

34 Do not get lost in the beauty of women,

35 Stay away from another man's wife,

36 In fact do not mettle in the affairs of womankind.[4]

37 For had I not seen Bilhah bathing in a covered place, I would not have fallen into this great iniquity.

38 For my mind taking in the thought of her nakedness haunted me, and I could not to sleep until I had wrought the abominable thing.[5]

Lust and pornography are not new conditions but have always been a struggle. Sex and womankind are 100% necessary to the very purpose of creation and man's destiny, but Reuben's warning stands. One must be on guard because these are powerful urges. Even King David was overcome and he was a prophet, beloved of the Lord.

39 For while Jacob our father had gone to Isaac his father, when we were in Eder, near to Ephrath in Bethlehem, Bilhah became drunk and was asleep uncovered in her chamber.

40 Having therefore gone in and beheld her nakedness, I wrought the impiety without her perceiving it, and leaving her sleeping departed.

41 And forthwith an angel of God revealed to my father concerning my impiety, and he came and mourned over me, and touched her no more.[6]

Reuben 2:1 Pay no heed, therefore, my children, to the beauty of women, nor set your mind on their affairs; but walk in singleness of heart in the fear of the Lord, and expend labour on good works, and on study and on your flocks, until the Lord gives you a wife, whom He will, that ye suffer not as I did.

2 For until my father's death I had not boldness to look in his face, or to speak to any of my brethren, because of the reproach.

3 Even until now my conscience causeth me anguish on account of my impiety.

4 And yet my father comforted me much, and prayed for me unto the Lord, that the anger of the Lord might pass from me, even as the Lord showed.

5 And thenceforth until now I have been on my guard and sinned not.

One hears this wise counsel from the Lord in regards to all egos, the fragile male one, and otherwise:

D&C 121:45 Let thy bowels also be full of charity towards all men, and to the household of faith, and let virtue garnish thy thoughts unceasingly; then shall thy confidence wax strong in the presence of God [and men]; and the doctrine of the priesthood shall distill upon thy soul as the dews from heaven.

In other words, a pure intent and love for mankind is the secret to bravery and inner peace.

Reuben 2:6 Therefore, my children, I say unto you, observe all things whatsoever I command you, and ye shall not sin.

7 For a pit unto the soul is the sin of fornication, separating it from God, and bringing it near to idols, because it deceiveth the mind and understanding, and leadeth down young men down to the grave before their time.[7]

8 For many hath fornication destroyed; because, though a man be old or noble, or rich or poor, he bringeth reproach upon himself with the sons of men and derision with Beliar.[8]

9 For ye heard regarding Joseph how he guarded himself from a woman, and purged his thoughts from all fornication, and found favour in the sight of God and men.

10 For the Egyptian woman did many things unto him, and summoned magicians, and offered him love potions, but the purpose of his soul admitted no evil desire.[9]

11 Therefore the God of your fathers delivered him from every evil and hidden death.

12 For if fornication overcomes not your mind, neither can Beliar overcome you.

Reuben's weakness for women was such a trial for him that he will next express it in words that are stronger than we might use. It does illustrate an important point: Men and women are weakest in their weaknesses. This is redundant but more complicated than it sounds. Wise children of God throw their weaknesses upon the altar of the Lord and beg Him for mercy and strength in the day of their trial. Fools shake their fist at God and say, "You made me this way! Thus my weaknesses are not my sins! You cannot hold me accountable for what I do in my weakness!" One senses Reuben's deep frustration here but one also sees his desire to understand it all and rise above it.

13 For evil are women, my children; and since they have no power or strength over man, they use wiles by outward attractions, that they may draw him to themselves.

14 And whom they cannot bewitch by outward attractions, him they overcome by craft.

15 For moreover, concerning them, the angel of the Lord told me, and taught me, that women are overcome by the spirit of fornication more than men, and in their heart they plot against men; and by means of their adornment they deceive first their minds, and by the glance of the eye instil the poison, and then through the accomplished act they take them captive.

16 For a woman cannot force a man openly, but by a harlot's bearing she beguiles him.[10]

17 Flee, therefore, fornication, my children, and command your wives and your daughters, that they adorn not their heads and faces to deceive the mind: because every woman who useth these wiles hath been reserved for eternal punishment.

18 For thus they allured the Watchers who were before the flood; for as these continually beheld them, they lusted after them, and they conceived the act in their mind; for they changed themselves into the shape of men, and appeared to them when they were with their husbands.

19 And the women lusting in their minds after their forms, gave birth to giants, for the Watchers appeared to them as reaching even unto heaven.[11]

20 Beware, therefore, of fornication; and if you wish to be pure in mind, guard your senses from every woman.

21 And command the women likewise not to associate with men, that they also may be pure in mind.

22 For constant meetings, even though the ungodly deed be not wrought, are to them an irremediable disease, and to us a destruction of Beliar and an eternal reproach.

23 For in fornication there is neither understanding nor godliness, and all jealousy dwelleth in the lust thereof.

24 Therefore, then I say unto you, ye will be jealous against the sons of Levi, and will seek to be exalted over them; but ye shall not be able.

25 For God will avenge them, and ye shall die by an evil death. For to Levi God gave the sovereignty and to Judah with him and to me also, and to Dan and Joseph, that we should be for rulers.[12]

26 Therefore I command you to hearken to Levi, because he shall know the law of the Lord, and shall give ordinances for judgement and shall sacrifice for

all Israel until the consummation of the times, as the anointed High Priest, of whom the Lord spoke.

27 I adjure you by the God of heaven to do truth each one unto his neighbour and to entertain love each one for his brother.

28 And draw ye near to Levi in humbleness, of heart, that ye may receive a blessing from his mouth.

29 For he shall bless Israel through Judah, because him hath the Lord chosen to be king over all the nation.

30 And bow down before his seed, for on our behalf his son will die in wars visible and invisible, and will be among you an eternal king.

A beautiful prophecy of the coming of the Lord Jesus Christ through the tribe of Judah.

31 And Reuben died, having given these commands to his sons. And they placed him in a coffin until they carried him up from Egypt, and buried him in Hebron in the cave where his father was.

Genesis 46:9 And the sons of Reuben; Hanoch, and Phallu, and Hezron, and Carmi.

LATTER-DAY LESSONS FROM FATHER REUBEN

I don't believe that it is possible to read the testimony of Reuben and not be deeply touched by his wisdom, his masculine experience, his candor and his humanity. It is a magnificent witness from the eldest son of Israel about the pitfalls and realities of a man's journey on Earth with all the ups and downs of life subjected to the council of the Lord and the whims of Lucifer. Reuben's lessons on true repentance fits the paradigm of Latter-day understanding perfectly. It is to me a testament of the correctness of the Lord's candor that: the more public the sin, the more public the confession. The more private the sin, the more private the confession." The point really is "an eye for an eye." If a brother sins against a brother, the righting of the sin is brother to brother (with the Lord as the third party). If a sin is between a woman and her community, then the righting of it is between her and the broader community. It is not necessary or required to publickly make a showing of a private sin. Not all sins need a bishop, but all sins do need a repentant heart, a contrite spirit, and the Lord. President Hinckley once gave a masterful sermon on overcoming sin. He effectively said (and so we paraphrase) that in overcoming a sin, the first step is to draw a line in the sand, and commit oneself to not exacerbating it.[13] Then set goals, day by day at first, then week by week, and build one's self up with humility and prayer, gaining strength and patience until one has overcome. I believe his ultimate point was that too often we just give up because we feel weak or worse we throw away the Lord to keep the sin. Drawing the line in the sand is important because Satan always attempts to get us to follow him down a slippery slop of increasing sin until we have lost all our rights and, if possible, become perdition, like he is.

By starting where you are, and making reasonable goals, such as: "Today, I will not sin and will call upon the Lord this day to help me conquer until tomorrow morning." One can find the strength to have success. If one is weak and says, "I will never commit sin again as long as I live," one may be setting himself up for continual failure. By keeping the Lord in the loop and leaning on Him as needed, one can find the strength to conquer in the long term. I found this to be brilliant and comforting advice.

The parental love of Jacob, forgiving his son and praying to the Lord on his behalf, is deeply touching. It is very interesting to see also the alternations in their stories and understandings. It furthers the contention that Reuben actually had sinned against his father, as well as Bilhah. In eastern thinking it was the same thing. Thus Jacob's forgiveness, and his going to the Lord on behalf of Reuben, fits perfectly with our understanding of repentance.

Note how even after Reuben's sin, he felt like he could never lift his head, and look his father in the eye, again. It dovetails perfectly with the Lord's statement to Joseph Smith:

D&C 121:45 ...let virtue garnish thy thoughts unceasingly; then shall thy confidence wax strong in the presence of God [and all men.]; and the doctrine of the priesthood shall distil upon thy soul as the dews from heaven.

This from the one who created us who knows how we work intrinsically. I would trust Him.

One of the more interesting insights that Reuben offers is how carrying the burden of a sin (and sometimes the guilt of it even after repentance) can be like a *hidden, living death*, to use his words. Reuben's ultimate lesson is a gift to his descendants: "Don't do the things I did and spend your life regretting it. It's just not worth it." Reuben lost much. Had he made different choices, he and his family would be greater in Israel today. He was the firstborn of Israel, heir to all the promises of Abraham, Isaac and Israel.[14] His name might have come after theirs, but today almost no one remembers him, and he was once the first of Israel's strength! Instead of the richest of blessings, this is what Father Israel left him in the end:

Genesis 49:3 Reuben, thou art my firstborn, my might, and the beginning of my strength, the excellency of dignity, and the excellency of power:

4 Unstable as water, thou shalt not excel; because thou wentest up to thy father's bed; then defiledst thou it: he went up to my couch.

Oh, that he could take that back. Moses would leave him some comfort when he blessed the tribes a second time. He said:

Deuteronomy 33:6 Let Reuben live, and not die; and let not his men be few.

Chapter Two

Simeon

And now, my children, hearken unto me and beware of the spirit of deceit and envy. Love each one his brother with a good heart, and the spirit of envy will withdraw from you. — *Simeon*

Simeon was the second son of Jacob and Leah. He was known for his strength. All of Jacob's sons were large, strong and handsome, so much so that Jacob lamented that his boys would be stolen and pressed into the service of some king's army. Simeon struggled with anger issues and envy; a dangerous combination for anyone. Here we learn that he was the instigator of the trouble against Joseph. It is useful to remember that until Joseph was born, Simeon's only real threat to power in the family was Reuben, whom he loved. When Joseph was born there was the nagging possibility that he was the true heir of Jacob, since his marriage to Leah had been a ruse. Certainly Joseph would have had claim if Reuben died.

Simeon 1:1 The copy of the words of Simeon, the things which he spake to his sons before he died, in the hundred and twentieth year of his life, at which time Joseph, his brother, died.

2 For when Simeon was sick, his sons came to visit him, and he strengthened himself and sat up and kissed them, and said:

3 Hearken, my children, to Simeon your father and I will declare unto you what things I have in my heart.

4 I was born of Jacob as my father's second son; and my mother Leah called me Simeon, because the Lord had heard her prayer [for a son].

Simeon and Simon mean "listen" and "heard."

5 Moreover, I became strong exceedingly; I shrank from no achievement nor was I afraid of ought. For my heart was hard, and my liver was immovable, and my bowels without compassion.

6 Because valour also has been given from the Most High to men in soul and body.

7 For in the time of my youth I was jealous in many things of Joseph, because my father loved him beyond all.

If Jacob had any fault, it was clear to all that he loved Rachel more than Leah, and Joseph more than any other son. While one cannot easily control whom we love, one must be careful of favoritism. Satan will always use that against us, particularly in a family. It is useful to follow the Father's model. He loves us all the same and what He offers to one, He offers to all. Jacob would have had a happier life had he been able to do that.

8 And I set my mind against my brother Joseph to destroy him because the prince of deceit sent forth the spirit of jealousy and blinded my mind, so that I regarded him not as a brother, nor did I spare even Jacob my father.

9 But his God and the God of his fathers sent forth His angel, and delivered Joseph out of my hands.

10 For when I went to Shechem to bring ointment for the flocks, and Reuben to Dothan, where were our necessaries and all our stores, Judah my brother sold him to the Ishmaelites.

Shechem was also the name of the prince of the Canaanites whom Simeon and Levi slew for raping their full sister Dinah. We will discover a very interesting twist on that story when Levi bares his witness next. It seems that Jacob's sons took over the land of Shechem after they had murdered all the men. It seems that some of the brothers liked to visit that area because there were suddenly a lot of widowed women.

We do get an insight here into Reuben's heart which furthers our assessment of him, despite his flaws, as being the best of Leah's sons.

Simeon 1:11 And when Reuben heard these things he was grieved, for he wished to restore him to his father.

12 But on hearing this I was exceedingly wroth against Judah in that he let Joseph go away alive, and for five months I continued wrathful against him.

13 But the Lord restrained me, and withheld from me the power of my hands; for my right hand was half withered for seven days.

Remember that Simeon was deeply proud of his physical strength and prowess. A man with no hands is not really a man who can use his body as the tool God intended. A man's strength is a source of his pride.

14 And I knew, my children, that because of Joseph this had befallen me, and I repented and wept; and I besought the Lord God that my hand might be restored and that I might hold aloof from all pollution and envy and from all folly.

15 For I knew that I had devised an evil thing before the Lord and Jacob my father, on account of Joseph my brother, in that I envied him.

How many times have we read thus in regards to our forebears. "I knew something was wrong, but I did it anyway." Oh that we might remember this. When we feel that something is wrong, don't do it. *Easier said then done, we all know.*

16 And now, my children, hearken unto me and beware of the spirit of deceit and envy.

17 For envy ruleth over the whole mind of a man, and suffereth him neither to eat nor to drink, nor to do any good thing. But it ever suggesteth to him to destroy him that he envieth; and so long as he that is envied flourisheth, he that envieth fadeth away.

18 Two years therefore I afflicted my soul with fasting in the fear of the Lord, and I learnt that deliverance from envy cometh by the fear of God.

This is Simeon's gift to us; the understanding through a life so lived that fearing and respecting the Lord is the cure for envy.

19 For if a man flee to the Lord, the evil spirit runneth away from him and his mind is lightened.

20 And henceforward he sympathiseth with him whom he envied and forgiveth those who are hostile to him, and so ceaseth from his envy.

Simeon 2:1 And my father asked concerning me, because he saw that I was sad; and I said unto him, I am pained in my liver.

2 For I mourned more than they all, because I was guilty of the selling of Joseph.

Part of the brothers' pain was the secret combination they had devised among themselves to keep the truth from their father and mothers.

3 And when we went down into Egypt, and he bound me as a spy, I knew that I was suffering justly, and I grieved not.

4 Now Joseph was a good man, and had the Spirit of God within him: being compassionate and pitiful, he bore no malice against me; but loved me even as the rest of his brethren.

5 Beware, therefore, my children, of all jealousy and envy, and walk in singleness of heart, that God may give you also grace and glory, and blessing upon your heads, even as ye saw in Joseph's case.

6 All his days he reproached us not concerning this thing, but loved us as his own soul, and beyond his own sons glorified us, and gave us riches, and cattle and fruits.

Note that Joseph never brought it up nor held it in his family's face, ever. That is amazing.

7 Do ye also, my children, love each one his brother with a good heart, and the spirit of envy will withdraw from you.

8 For this maketh savage the soul and destroyeth the body; it causeth anger and war in the mind, and stirreth up unto deeds of blood, and leadeth the mind into frenzy, and causeth tumult to the soul and trembling to the body.

9 For even in sleep malicious jealousy gnaweth, and with wicked spirits disturbeth the soul, and causeth the body to be troubled, and waketh the mind from sleep in confusion; and as a wicked and poisonous spirit, so appeareth it to men.

10 Therefore was Joseph comely in appearance, and goodly to look upon, because no wickedness dwelt in him; for some of the trouble of the spirit the face manifesteth.

President Gordon B. Hinckley said the same thing to the church in one of his many memorable addresses. Living the gospel makes a person handsome or beautiful.

11 And now, my children, make your hearts good before the Lord, and your ways straight before men, and ye shall find grace before the Lord and men.

12 Beware, therefore, of fornication, for fornication is mother of all evils, separating from God, and bringing near to Beliar.

13 For I have seen it inscribed in the writing of Enoch that your sons shall be corrupted in fornication, and shall do harm to the sons of Levi with the sword.

14 But they shall not be able to withstand Levi; for he shall wage the war of the Lord, and shall conquer all your hosts.

15 And they shall be few in number, divided in Levi and Judah, and there shall be none of you for sovereignty, even as also our father prophesied in his blessings.

Simeon was saying that his tribe would not excel to the throne like Judah, nor to the priesthood authority like Levi. They were also not heir to the birthright, thus the best thing they could do would be to support those tribes that did bare the greater calling. It takes some a long time to learn this. As much as some younger men aspire to leadership in the church, or as much as some women desire to be men, all of this is folly. The Lord doesn't require some things of all of us and in that wise men and women rejoice. If I am not called to the burden of Levi, then I am free to pursue goodness and life choices of my own. Why would I not want to be free to choose my own good works? Why would I want to aspire to another's burden before the Lord? Where none is given, none is required. See our supplemental feast on *Gad* for more on this.

Simeon 3:1 Behold I have told you all things, that I may be acquitted of your sin.

2 Now, if ye remove from you your envy and all stiff-neckedness, as a rose shall my bones flourish in Israel, and as a lily my flesh in Jacob, and my odour

shall be as the odour of Lebanon; and as cedars shall holy ones be multiplied from me for ever, and their branches shall stretch afar off.

3 Then shall perish the seed of Canaan, and a remnant shall not be unto Amalek, and all the Philistines shall perish, and all Hittites [Chaldeans] shall be utterly destroyed.

4 Then shall fail the land of Ham, and all the people shall perish.

5 Then shall all the earth rest from trouble, and all the world under heaven from war.

6 Then the Mighty One of Israel shall glorify Shem.

7 For the Lord God shall appear on earth, and Himself save men,

8 Then shall all the spirits of deceit be given to be trodden under foot, and men shall rule over wicked spirits.

9 Then shall I arise in joy and will bless the Most High because of his marvellous works, because God hath taken a body and eaten with men and saved men.

10 And now, my children, obey Levi and Judah, and be not lifted up against these two tribes, for from them shall arise unto you the salvation of God.

11 For the Lord shall raise up from Levi as it were a High Priest, and from Judah as it were a King, God and man, He shall save all the Gentiles and the race of Israel.

He is speaking about Moses, Aaron, John the Baptist, and Jesus Christ.

12 Therefore I give you these commands that ye also may command your children, that they may observe them throughout their generations.

13 And when Simeon had made an end of commanding his sons, he slept with his fathers, an hundred and twenty years old.

14 And they laid him in a wooden coffin, to take up his bones to Hebron. And they took them up secretly during a war of the Egyptians.[15] For the bones of Joseph the Egyptians guarded in the tombs of the kings for they feared that he would leave them.

15 For the sorcerers told them, that on the departure of the bones of Joseph there should be throughout all the land darkness and gloom, and an exceeding

great plague to the Egyptians, so that even with a lamp a man should not recognize his brother.

16 And the sons of Simeon bewailed their father.

17 And they were in Egypt until the day of their departure by the hand of Moses.

Genesis 46:10 And the sons of Simeon; Jemuel, and Jamin, and Ohad, and Jachin, and Zohar, and Shaul the son of a Canaanitish woman.

LATTER-DAY LESSONS FROM FATHER SIMEON

Simeon shares with us how it is impossible in this life to not have Satan use our strengths against us. We know that he uses our weaknesses against us. What we learn from Simeon is that Satan is able to turn our strengths into a weaknesses. The Lord has said that He can mentor our weaknesses until they became our strengths. In fact, He commands us to come to Him with our weaknesses and He will make us strong. By commanding us to come, it is our invitation and promise that the Lord will receive us. He always keeps His word. Any man or woman who comes to the Lord with his weakness, will not be turned away.

His analyzation on envy and the human soul is masterful; pointing out how all of the good works we might do in this life to gain our own crown are wasted away in worrying about the success of another. Indeed this was the trap that Satan used to destroy Cain. Simeon says that the only escape is to be god-fearing. We know that god-fearing leads to respect and, as one comes to see the good fruits of respecting God in his life, those good fruits lead to love. In other words, if you don't have it in your heart now to love God, try respecting Him and see if He doesn't give you more than enough reason to love Him. You will discover that all good things come from Him, because He already loves you.

Simeon wants his sons to know that legacy is important. Since his tribe was not called to be kings, priests or saviours on Mount Zion (at least not until the Messianic Age), they are still able to claim great honors in Israel by giving their legacy of support. This is, to a large degree, why learning not to envy was to be so important in Simeon's clan. Those of us who are not called to positions of great power or responsibility in this life, are also not accountable for those great powers or responsibilities. One cannot help but wonder if King David could have seen the beginning from the end, if he would have accepted the assignment of king? *The Book of Gad the Seer,* which is also available in this series, illustrates this point brilliantly when Hiram King of Tyre asks King David about what is required of him and his non-Israeli kingdom. Simeon admits to his children, his amazement that Joseph never spoke, nor condemned, nor said anything to him about the murder attempt. We do know from Genesis that Joseph threw Simeon in prison as a hostage while the brothers went home to fetch Benjamin. The reason for Simeon being so-called, randomly selected as prisoner now makes sense. Rabbinic tradition does say that Joseph let Simeon out after 3 days and treated him like a house guest under guard during the several months he was left there. Simeon's repentance was such that he admits he deserved it.

Simeon echos Reuben's warning about the dangers of fornication. In fact, when the heavenly histories of Earth's days are opened will we see how Lucifer has used fornication, with its accompanying shame to build his kingdom among us. He or she who flees from this sin, places an armor about himself that is difficult to penetrate.

At Simeon's death, he was considered worthy to be buried with the patriarchs in Hebron. We do get the important clue that there were wars beginning in the lands in those days. Followers of our *Gospel Feast Series* know that with the death of Nimrod particularly, and the withdrawal of Israel from the land, most definitely, a vacuum of power was created. This instability coupled with the great famine, made the world a very dangerous place. The clue here, along with others in our *Gospel Feast Series*, explains the Lord's need for Joseph in Egypt and why he took young Israel there in the first place. Egypt, during these terrible years of death and famine, was safe.

When Israel blessed Simeon, he merged the blessing with Levi's. We will save those words for our summation after Levi.

Tu cum fratre sequente procul fugias, apage-sis: 2.
Quid mihi, quid tecum sanguinolente LEVI?

Chapter Three

Levi

My children, choose for yourselves either the light or the darkness,
either the law of the Lord or the works of Beliar. — Levi

Levi was the third son of Jacob and Leah. His testimony is extremely interesting in that it explains who he was, why the Lord chose him, and why in the end he was not punished for the murder of the men of Shechem; which has always puzzled the Biblical reader. As we shall see, Levi was both a mystic, a dreamer of dreams like Joseph, and a prophet. In the end Joseph was greater because he was also an interpreter of dreams and was a seer.

Levi 1:1 The copy of the words of Levi, the things which he ordained unto his sons, according to all that they should do, and what things should befall them until the day of judgement.

2 He was sound in health when he called them to him; for it had been revealed to him that he should die.

3 And when they were gathered together he said to them:

4 I, Levi, was born in Haran, and I came with my father to Shechem.

5 And I was young, about twenty years of age, when, with Simeon, I wrought vengeance on Hamor for our sister Dinah.

6 And when I was feeding the flocks in Abel-Maul, the spirit of understanding of the Lord came upon me, and I saw all men corrupting their way, and that unrighteousness had built for itself walls, and lawlessness sat upon towers.[16]

7 And I was grieving for the race of the sons of men, and I prayed to the Lord that I might be saved.

8 Then there fell upon me a sleep, and I beheld a high mountain, and I was upon it.

9 And behold the heavens were opened, and an angel of God said to me, "Levi, enter."

10 And I entered from the first heaven, and I saw there a great sea hanging.

11 And further I saw a second heaven far brighter and more brilliant, for there was a boundless light also therein,

12 And I said to the angel, "Why is this so?" And the angel said to me, "Marvel not at this, for thou shalt see another heaven more brilliant and incomparable.

13 And when thou hast ascended thither, Thou shalt stand near the Lord, and shalt be His minister, and shalt, declare His mysteries to men, and shalt proclaim concerning Him that shall redeem Israel.

14 And by thee and Judah shall the Lord appear among men, saving every race of men.

Ultimately this would be John the Baptist and Jesus Christ. It was because of clearly spoken promises like this that were known in Israel, that the people were waiting and watching for the Messiah. This is why they went out to John in the desert and took his selection of Jesus of Nazareth as the Lamb very seriously. Books such as Levi's here were tossed aside by the Judaic after the rejection of Jesus Christ because these books could not be explained post-Hasmonean protectorate.

Levi 1:15 And from the Lord's portion shall be thy life, and He shall be thy field and vineyard, and fruits, gold, and silver.

This changes our understanding of the Lord's mission for Levi. Christianity too often teaches that Levi came into importance due to the national sin at Sinai, but this book is saying that the Lord had always intended for one of the tribes to be full time priests, officiating the needs of temporal salvation for the greater nation who would function in their own homes and families under a patriarchal order. Suddenly this makes a great deal of sense, fits with prophetic books such as *Ezekiel* and explains why Adam, Enoch, Noah, Shem and Abraham functioned as Melchizedek-Father priests.

Levi will next experience a heavenly schemata that no one but Joseph Smith could have foreseen. Note the number of heavens here and how they are described. Where have you heard this before?

Levi 1:16 Hear, therefore, regarding the heavens which have been shown to thee.

17 The lowest is for this cause gloomy unto thee, in that it beholds all the unrighteous deeds of men.

18 And it has fire, snow, and ice made ready for the day of judgement, in the righteous judgement of God; for in it are all the spirits of the retributions for vengeance on men.

19 And in the second are the hosts of the armies which are ordained for the day of judgement, to work vengeance on the spirits of deceit and of Beliar.

20 And above them are the holy ones.

21 And in the highest of all dwelleth the Great Glory, far above all holiness.

22 In the heaven next to it are the archangels, who minister and make propitiation to the Lord for all the sins of ignorance of the righteous;

23 Offering to the Lord a sweet smelling savour, a reasonable and a bloodless offering.

24 And in the heaven below this are the angels who bear answers to the angels of the presence of the Lord.

25 And in the heaven next to this are thrones and dominions, in which always they offer praise to God.

26 When, therefore, the Lord looketh upon us, all of us are shaken; yea, the heavens, and the earth, and the abysses are shaken at the presence of His majesty.

27 But the sons of men, having no perception of these things, sin and provoke the Most High.

One man did have a "perception of these things" and explained them more clearly than this. See *Doctrine & Covenants 76* for more on the "many mansions of the Father."

Levi 2:1 Now, therefore, know that the Lord shall execute judgement upon the sons of men.

2 Because when the rocks are being rent, and the sun quenched, and the waters dried up, and the fire cowering, and all creation troubled, and the invisible spirits melting away, and the very world of the dead spoiled through the visitations of the Most High, men will still not believe but will persist in their iniquity.

3 On this account with punishment shall they be judged.

4 Therefore the Most High hath heard thy prayer, to separate thee from iniquity, and that thou shouldst become to Him a son, and a servant, and a minister of His presence.

5 The light of knowledge shalt thou light up in Jacob, and as the sun shalt thou be to all the seed of Israel.

6 And there shall be given to thee a blessing, and to all thy seed until the Lord shall visit all the Nations in His tender mercies for ever.

7 And therefore there have been given to thee counsel and understanding, that thou mightest instruct thy sons concerning this;

8 Because they that bless Him [Jesus] shall be blessed, and they that curse Him shall perish."

9 And thereupon the angel opened to me the gates of heaven, and I saw the holy temple, and upon a throne of glory the Most High.

10 And He said to me: "Levi, I have given thee the blessing of the priesthood until I come and sojourn in the midst of Israel."

And the Levitical order did continue, with more or less holiness, from Levi to John the Baptist. See *Vol. 4* on *Zechariah* for more on the importance of the Baptist to the earthly ministry of the Saviour.

11 Then the angel brought me down to the earth, and gave me a shield and a sword, and said to me: Execute vengeance on Shechem because of Dinah, thy sister, and I will be with thee because the Lord hath sent me.

12 And I destroyed at that time the sons of Hamor, as it is written in the heavenly tables.

13 And I said to him: "I pray thee, O Lord, tell me Thy name, that I may call upon Thee in a day of tribulation."

14 And he said: "I am the angel who intercedeth for the nation of Israel that they may not be smitten utterly, for every evil spirit attacketh it."

15 And after these things I awaked, and blessed the Most High, and the angel who intercedeth for the nation of Israel and for all the righteous.

Levi 3:1 And when I was going home to my father, I found a brazen shield; wherefore also the name of the mountain is Aspis, which is near Gebal, to the south of Abila.

2 And I kept these words in my heart. And after this I counselled my father, and Reuben my brother, to bid the sons of Hamor not to be circumcised; for I was zealous because of the abomination which they had wrought on my sister.

3 And I slew Shechem first, and Simeon slew Hamor. And after this my brothers came and smote that city with the edge of the sword.

4 And my father heard these things and was wroth, and he was grieved in that they had received the circumcision, and after that had been put to death, and in his deathbed blessings he looked amiss upon us.

5 For we sinned because we had done this thing against his will, and he was sick on that day.

6 But I saw that the sentence of God was for evil upon Shechem; for they sought to do to Sarah and Rebecca as they had done to Dinah our sister, but the Lord prevented them.

This is an important insight. These are the same people who tried to steal both Sarah and Rebekah from Abraham and Isaac. These had a practice of murdering husbands and stealing women. The Lord had finally had enough of it when Dinah was raped by their crown prince.[17]

7 And they persecuted Abraham our father when he was a stranger, and they vexed his flocks when they were big with young; and Eblaen, who was born in his house, they most shamefully handled.

8 And thus they did to all strangers, taking away their wives by force, and then banishing their husbands.

9 But the wrath of the Lord came upon them to the uttermost.

10 And I said to my father Jacob: "By thee will the Lord despoil the Canaanites, and will give their land to thee and to thy seed after thee.

11 For from this day forward shall Shechem be called a city of imbeciles; for as a man mocketh a fool, so did we mock them.

12 Because also they had wrought folly in Israel by defiling my sister." And we departed and came to Bethel.

THE VISION OF LEVI DRESSED IN THE ROBES OF HOLINESS

13 And there again I saw a vision as the former, after we had spent there seventy days.

14 And I saw seven men in white raiment saying unto me: "Arise, put on the robe of the priesthood, and the crown of righteousness, and the breastplate of understanding, and the garment of truth, and the crowned turban of faith on your head, and the ephod of prophecy.

15 And they severally carried these things and put them on me, and said unto me: From henceforth become a priest of the Lord, thou and thy seed for ever.

16 And the first anointed me with holy oil, and gave to me the staff of judgement.

17 The second washed me with pure water, and fed me with bread and wine even the most holy things, and clad me with a holy and glorious robe.

18 The third clothed me with a linen vestment like an ephod.

19 The fourth put round me a girdle like unto purple.

20 The fifth gave me a branch of rich olive.

21 The sixth placed a crown on my head.

22 The seventh placed on my head a diadem of priesthood, and filled my hands with incense, that I might serve as priest to the Lord God.

23 And they said to me: Levi, thy seed shall be divided into three offices, for a sign of the glory of the Lord who is to come.

24 And the first portion shall be great; yea, greater than it shall none be.

This was Moses and Aaron, and possibly Phineas who tradition whispers may have been Elijah.

25 The second shall be in the priesthood.

These were the Levites and there were many great ones like Samuel, Nathan, Gad and Zadok, and other not so great ones.

26 And the third shall be called by a new name, because a king shall arise in Judah, and shall establish a new priesthood, after the fashion of the Nations.

This is Jesus Christ, who did give His order a new name and did establish a new priesthood which was after the order of Adam, Noah (the nations) and Shem who was Melchizedek.

27 And His presence is beloved, as a prophet of the Most High, of the seed of Abraham our father.

Beloved here is a play on the name David. Jesus Christ was called the "Son of David."

28 Therefore, every desirable thing in Israel shall be for thee and for thy seed, and ye shall eat everything fair to look upon, and the table of the Lord shall thy seed apportion.

29 And some of them shall be high priests, and judges, and scribes; for by their mouth shall the holy place be guarded."

30 And when I awoke, I understood that this dream was like the first dream. And I hid this also in my heart, and told it not to any man upon the earth.

Joseph's mistake had been to blab his visions to everyone which only cast pearls before swine. Levi is keeping these in his heart until now when he shares them with his children.

31 And after two days I and Judah went up with our father Jacob to Isaac our father's father.

32 And my father's father blessed me according to all the words of the visions which I had seen. And he would not come with us to Bethel.

This is Levi's way of saying that he knows his vision was true because Isaac's blessing confirmed what he had been shown privately.

33 And when we came to Bethel, my father saw a vision concerning me, that I should be their full-time priest unto God.

34 And he rose up early in the morning, and paid tithes of all to the Lord through me. And so we came to Hebron to dwell there.

35 And Isaac called me continually to put me in remembrance of the law of the Lord, even as the angel of the Lord showed unto me.

36 And he taught me the law of the priesthood of sacrifices, whole burnt-offerings, first-fruits, freewill-offerings, peace-offerings.

37 And each day he was instructing me, and was busied on my behalf before the Lord, and said to me: Beware of the spirit of fornication; for this shall continue and shall by thy seed pollute the holy place.

38 Take, therefore, to thyself a wife without blemish or pollution, while yet thou are young, and not of the race of strange nations.

39 And before entering into the holy place, bathe; and when thou offerest the sacrifice, wash; and again, when thou finishest the sacrifice, wash.

40 Of twelve trees having leaves offer to the Lord, as Abraham taught me also.

41 And of every clean beast and bird offer a sacrifice to the Lord.

42 And of all thy first-fruits and of wine offer the first, as a sacrifice to the Lord God; and every sacrifice thou shalt salt with salt.

43 Now, therefore, observe whatsoever I command you, children; for whatsoever things I have heard from my fathers I have declared unto you.

44 And behold I am clear from your ungodliness and transgression, which ye shall commit in the end of the ages against the Saviour of the world, the Messiah, acting godlessly, deceiving Israel, and stirring up against it great evils from the Lord.

45 And ye shall deal lawlessly together with Israel, so He shall not bear with Jerusalem because of your wickedness; but the veil of the temple shall be rent, so as not to cover your shame.[18]

46 And ye shall be scattered as captives among the Gentiles, and shall be for a reproach and for a curse there.

47 For the house which the Lord shall choose shall be called Jerusalem, as is contained in the book of Enoch the righteous.

48 Therefore when I took a wife I was twenty-eight years old, and her name was Melcha.

49 And she conceived and bare a son, and I called his name Gersam, for we were sojourners in our land.

50 And I saw concerning him, that he would not be in the first rank.

51 And Kohath was born in the thirty-fifth year of my life, towards sunrise.

52 And I saw in a vision that he was standing on high in the midst of all the congregation.

53 Therefore I called his name Kohath which is, beginning of majesty and instruction.

Were it not for the *Dead Sea Scrolls*, and this book we would know nothing whatsoever about Kohath.

54 And she bare me a third son, in the fortieth year of my life; and since his mother bare him with difficulty, I called him Merari, that is, 'my bitterness,' because he also was like to die.

55 And my daughter Jochebed was born in Egypt, in my sixty-fourth year, for I was renowned then in the midst of my brethren.

Jochebed was Moses's mother. She would marry her nephew Amram. Prohibition against marrying close relatives did not come into effect until the Mosaic Law a few generations later.

56 And Gersam took a wife, and she bare to him Lomni and Semei. And the sons of Kohath, Amram, Issachar, Hebron, and Ozeel. And the sons of Merari, Mooli, and Mouses.

57 And in the ninety-fourth year Amram took Jochebed my daughter to him to wife, for they were born in one day, he and my daughter.

58 Eight years old was I when I went into the land of Canaan, and eighteen years when I slew Shechem, and at nineteen years I became priest, and at twenty-eight years I took a wife, and at forty-eight I went into Egypt.

59 And behold, my children, ye are a third generation. In my hundred and eighteenth year Joseph died.

Levi 4:1 And now, my children, I command you: Fear the Lord your God with your whole heart, and walk in simplicity according to all His law.

2 And do ye also teach your children to read and write and the Alef-bet, that they may have understanding all their life, reading unceasingly the law of God.

3 For every one that knoweth the law of the Lord shall be honoured, and shall not be a stranger whithersoever he goeth.

4 Yea, many friends shall he gain more than his parents, and many men shall desire to serve him, and to hear the law from his mouth.

5 Work righteousness, therefore, my children, upon the earth, that ye may have it as a treasure in heaven.

6 And sow good things in your souls, that ye may find them in your life.

7 But if ye sow evil things, ye shall reap every trouble and affliction.

8 Get wisdom in the fear of God with diligence; for though there be a leading into captivity, and cities and lands be destroyed, and gold and silver and every possession perish, the wisdom of the wise nought can take away, save the blindness of ungodliness, and the callousness that comes of sin.

9 For if one keep oneself from these evil things, then even among his enemies shall wisdom be a glory to him, and in a strange country a fatherland, and in the midst of foes shall prove a friend.

10 Whosoever teaches noble things and does them, shall be enthroned with kings, as was also Joseph my brother.

This is a beautiful promise based on the experience of our Father Joseph. Knowing the law of God, practicing it openly and teaching the same will save a man wherever he is.

THE PROPHECY OF LEVI

Levi 4:11 Therefore, my children, I have learnt that at the end of the ages ye will transgress against the Lord, stretching out hands to wickedness against Him; and to all the Gentiles shall ye become a scorn.

12 For our father Israel is pure from the transgressions of the chief priests [who shall lay their hands upon the Saviour of the world].

13 For as the heaven is purer in the Lord's sight than the earth, so also be ye, the lights of Israel, purer than all the Nations.

14 But if ye be darkened through transgressions, what, therefore, will all the Gentiles do living in blindness?

15 Yea, ye shall bring a curse upon our race, because the light of the law which was given for to lighten every man this ye desire to destroy by teaching commandments contrary to the ordinances of God.

16 The offerings of the Lord ye shall rob, and from His portion shall ye steal choice portions, eating them contemptuously with harlots.

17 And out of covetousness ye shall teach the commandments of the Lord, wedded women shall ye pollute, and the virgins of Jerusalem shall ye defile; and with harlots and adulteresses shall ye be joined, and the daughters of the Gentiles shall ye take to wife, purifying them with an unlawful purification; and your union shall be like unto Sodom and Gomorrah,

18 And ye shall be puffed up because of your priesthood, lifting yourselves up against men, and not only so, but also against the commands of God.

19 For ye shall contemn the holy things with jests and laughter.

20 Therefore the temple, which the Lord shall choose, shall be laid waste through your uncleanness, and ye shall be captives throughout all nations.

21 And ye shall be an abomination unto them, and ye shall receive reproach and everlasting shame from the righteous judgement of God.

22 And all who hate you shall rejoice at your destruction.

All of this came to pass. The sin of Israel became the justification in the eyes of the nation to abhor them. The Ten Tribes escaped in the end, leaving Judah to bear the brunt of this terrible curse.

23 And if you were not to receive mercy through Abraham, Isaac, and Jacob, our fathers, not one of our seed should be left upon the earth.

In other words the promise would be honored because of the fathers and not because of anything they had done.

24 And now I have learnt that for seventy weeks ye shall go astray, and profane the priesthood, and pollute the sacrifices.

25 And ye shall make void the law, and set at nought the words of the prophets by evil perverseness.

26 And ye shall persecute righteous men, and hate the godly; the words of the faithful shall ye abhor.

27 And a man who reneweth the law in the power of the Most High, ye shall call a deceiver; and at last ye shall rush upon him to slay him, not knowing his dignity, taking innocent blood through wickedness upon your heads.

28 And your holy places shall be laid waste even to the ground because of him.

This was Jesus Christ.

29 And ye shall have no place that is clean; but ye shall be among the Gentiles a curse and a dispersion until He shall again visit you, and in pity shall receive you through faith and water.

When the Jews lost their temple, they lost their culture too and were scattered among the nations. Through a new commission and a new cleansing baptism, they will return in the Lord's own way and time.

THE PROPHECY OF THE PRIESTHOOD

The clarity of this prophecy in scripture is a rarity. What it proves is that prophecies and patriarchal blessings given in private can be clearer than those given for the perusal and mockery of the world, such as Daniel's words given in exile.

Levi 5:1 And whereas ye have heard concerning the seventy weeks, hear also concerning the priesthood. For in each jubilee there shall be a priesthood.

2 And in the first jubilee, the first who is anointed to the priesthood shall be great, and shall speak to God as to a father.

3 And his priesthood shall be perfect with the Lord, and in the day of his gladness shall he arise for the salvation of the world.

4 In the second jubilee, he that is anointed shall be conceived in the sorrow of beloved ones; and his priesthood shall be honoured and shall be glorified by all.

5 And the third priest shall he taken hold of by sorrow.

6 And the fourth shall be in pain, because unrighteousness shall gather itself against him exceedingly, and all Israel shall hate each one his neighbour.

7 The fifth shall be taken hold of by darkness. Likewise also the sixth and the seventh.

8 And in the seventh shall, be such pollution as I cannot express before men, for they shall know it who do these things.

9 Therefore shall they be taken captive and become a prey, and their land and their substance shall be destroyed.

That was the day of Jeremiah and Ezekiel.

10 And in the fifth week they shall return to their desolate country, and shall renew the house of the Lord.

This would be High Priest Joshua, Haggai, Zechariah, and Ezra.

11 And in the seventh week shall become priests, who are idolaters, adulterers, lovers of money, proud, lawless, lascivious, abusers of children and beasts.

12 And after their punishment shall have come from the Lord, the priesthood shall fail.

The Levitical Order fell with the murder of John the Baptist. This meant to the Jews, who understood it, that in the days of this loss, they were to look for the Messiah to be the new priest. John the Baptist was a sign, the one crying in the wilderness, and the people knew it.

13 Then shall the Lord raise up a new priest.

Jesus the Christ, after the order of Melchizedek. Note what is said of him:

14 And to him all the words of the Lord shall be revealed; and he shall execute a righteous judgement upon the earth for a multitude of days.

15 And his star shall arise in heaven as of a king.

16 Lighting up the light of knowledge as the sun the day, and he shall be magnified in the world.

17 He shall shine forth as the sun on the earth, and shall remove all darkness from under heaven, and there shall be peace in all the earth.

18 The heavens shall exult in his days, and the earth shall be glad, and the clouds shall rejoice;

19 And the knowledge of the Lord shall be poured forth upon the earth, as the water of the seas;

20 And the angels of the glory of the presence of the Lord shall be glad in him.

21 The heavens shall be opened, and from the temple of glory shall come upon him sanctification, with the Father's voice as from Abraham to Isaac.

22 And the glory of the Most High shall be uttered over him, and the spirit of understanding and sanctification shall rest upon him in the water.

23 For he shall give the majesty of the Lord to His sons in truth for evermore;

24 And there shall none succeed him for all generations for ever.

Scriptures like this, which were had among the people in Jesus's day, prove the contention of Joseph Smith that more of the Gospel was known anciently than we are apt to believe today.

Peter and the 12 Apostles would next be mentioned. This is important because they were not Levites but functioned under the higher Priesthood order of the Messiah.

25 And in his priesthood the Gentiles shall be multiplied in knowledge upon the earth, and enlightened through the grace of the Lord. In his priesthood shall sin come to an end, and the lawless shall cease to do evil.

26 And he shall open the gates of paradise, and shall remove the threatening sword against Adam, and he shall give to the saints to eat from the tree of life, and the spirit of holiness shall be on them.

27 And Beliar shall be bound by him, and he shall give power to His children to tread upon the evil spirits.

28 And the Lord shall rejoice in His children, and be well pleased in His beloved ones for ever.

29 Then shall Abraham and Isaac and Jacob exult, and I will be glad, and all the saints shall clothe themselves with joy.

This is the Great Wedding we are waiting for even now.

30 And now, my children, ye have heard all; choose, therefore, for yourselves either the light or the darkness, either the law of the Lord or the works of Beliar.

31 And his sons answered him., saying, Before the Lord we will walk according to His law.

32 And their father said unto them, The Lord is witness, and His angels are witnesses, and ye are witnesses, and I am witness, concerning the word of your mouth.

33 And his sons said unto him: We are witnesses.

34 And thus Levi ceased commanding his sons; and he stretched out his feet on the bed, and was gathered to his fathers, after he had lived a hundred and thirty-seven years.

35 And they laid him in a coffin, and afterwards they buried him in Hebron, with Abraham, Isaac, and Jacob.

Genesis 46:11 And the sons of Levi; Gershon, Kohath, and Merari.

LATTER-DAY LESSONS FROM FATHER LEVI

Fragments of Levi's testimony were some of the lengthiest found among the *Dead Sea Scrolls*. His witness shatters Biblical commentary and current understand more than any other testimony of the sons of Israel, which may be why the Lord preserved such a large piece of it. Note this well, Levi's testimony would be nonsensical and worthless outside the Restored Gospel at the hands of Joseph Smith. Levi's testimony shakes modern concepts of Judaism and secular christianity. It also challenges some simplistic Mormon concepts (ones we might call uninspired Sunday School answers) while at the same time testifying of the accuracy of Joseph Smith's discourses and his powers as a seer. Let's explore some of these:

I have enjoyed playing the following word game with my Jewish friends from time to time. I ask then, "Who was the greatest Jew?" Most will say, "Moses." Then I point out that Moses was not a Jew but a Levite. Some will answer, "Abraham." Then I will say, "But Abraham was Judah's great grandfather, how can he be a Jew? He was a Hebrew." Christians know the answer that the greatest Jew of all is Jesus Christ. In the end, the game falls apart when you are forced to admit that today when we say "Jew" we really mean the Jewish faith and culture since only the Tribe of Judah remains culturally intact, but it's fun.

All of this illustrates an important point. How many times have you been taught that the *Levitical Order of the Priesthood* didn't exist until the *Melchizedek Order* was divided at the debacle of the Golden Calf? Every four years? *The Testimony of Levi* explains that having a Tribe of Priests set apart to maintain the greater priestly duties of Zion was ALWAYS the Lord's plan. This is huge, earth-shattering information! Suddenly Moses and Aaron make sense.

Aaron wasn't called because all the males of Israel were suddenly unworthy to officiate, and he was mostly worthy. No! Aaron was called because he was the eldest living son of Amram, who was the eldest living son of Kohath, so was the eldest, worthy living son of Levi! All the males of Israel were to be elders, high priests, sages and fathers in Israel but they blew it.

The Melchizedek authority is patriarchal, fraternal, and parental, we know that. Abraham, Isaac, Jacob, Noah, Shem, and Enoch, Adam, Jehovah, and Elohim are all Fathers and Husbands. They gain their power to lead and minister beneath Zion's canopy held down by stakes. It is another astounding proof of Joseph Smith's ministry. The symbolism in Latter-day Zion is perfectly *Old Testament*.

Melchizedek authority is a father's authority, ordained and bestowed by one with power to grant it, but the spiritual and temporal needs of the kingdom need full-time priests. This is why Joseph stated that the right to a Bishopric would ultimately reside with the sons of Levi. So how do we get around this today? The Lord thought of that as well. Are you surprised? Of course not. Our God is just that great!

Doctrine & Covenants 84:18 And the Lord confirmed a priesthood also upon Aaron and his seed, throughout all their generations, which priesthood also continueth and abideth forever with the priesthood which is after the holiest order of God...

33 For whoso is faithful unto the obtaining these two priesthoods of which I have spoken, and the magnifying their calling, are sanctified by the Spirit unto the renewing of their bodies.

34 They become the sons of Moses and of Aaron and the seed of Abraham, and the church and kingdom, and the elect of God.

Who are the sons of Levi? You are. This is why, I believe, Ezekiel further clarifies which sons of Levi will be administrating the temporal needs of the 3rd Temple at Jerusalem. Those will be the Levitical sons of Zadok. See *Ezekiel & the Millennial Reign of Christ, Vol. 5 in our Gospel Feast Series* for more.

Levi testifies that there is indeed many mansions in our Father's house; another concept forgotten until the Restoration. Judaism and Christianity teach of Heaven or Hell, good place or bad place. It was by the Spirit that the Latter-Day Saints realized that such a scenario was patently unfair, nor was it the saying of Jesus Christ during his ministry. Mormons speak of 3 mansions, with the third being the Celestial Kingdom which also has 3 houses. If one adds to this Outer Darkness, one does indeed come to Levi's 7 heavens, but it is also possible that Levi was counting either the Earth or the heaven's above which were sometimes called "heaven" anciently. This is not outside

Mormonism either, as we are taught that this world is a telestial kingdom, merely one level above Outer Darkness. Being at the farthest spiral from the light at the center or our galaxy, it is easy to see how we are but one step ahead of the Outer darkness of lonely space.

Levi's sad witness of the crucifixion of the Messiah, when he said that his sons would destroy the Son of God, is in perfect keeping with the Lord's fairness. Levi's sons had enough forewarning to teach their children and change their individual path. That they chose not to do so, and to keep these records from some of the people in time, explains the Lord's wrath in later books such as *Ezekiel, Haggai,* and *Isaiah.*

Of the many interesting truths given by Levi's testimony two jump out. A correct guidepost for understanding the Jubilee Calendar and the fact that it was God who ordained the death of the males of Shechem for defiling Dinah. The Bible account alone portrays this as a dastardly deed, murderous and cunning, but Levi says he was commanded to do it by God, just as Joshua would later be ordered to cleanse the land. He explains God's rationale for such clearly. He further explains his father's frustration. The Bible makes it appear that Jacob is angry about the murder, but Levi clarifies that it's the deception of having the men take part in Abraham's covenant of circumcision then killing them that is the problem. This makes a lot more sense. These men had raped Dinah and would have raped Sarah and Rebekah after killing the prophets of God. Levi admits that his father was angry about that but we also find that Levi begged Israel not to offer them the covenant in the first place. Jacob would never forget this and even in his final blessing, he recounted it:

Genesis 49:5 Simeon and Levi are brethren; instruments of cruelty are in their habitations.

6 O my soul, come not thou into their secret; unto their assembly, mine honour, be not thou united: for in their anger they slew a man, and in their selfwill they digged down a wall.

7 Cursed be their anger, for it was fierce; and their wrath, for it was cruel: I will divide them in Jacob, and scatter them in Israel.

And Moses:

Deuteronomy 33:8 Let thy Thummim and thy Urim be with thy holy one,...

10 They shall teach Jacob thy judgments, and Israel thy law: they shall put incense before thee, and whole burnt sacrifice upon thine altar.

11 Bless, Lord, his substance, and accept the work of his hands: smite through the loins of them that rise against him, and of them that hate him, that they rise not again.

Judah Propositions to Tamar by Emile Vernet, 1840.

Chapter Four

Judah

My children, be not drunk with wine; for wine turneth the mind away from the truth, and inspires the passion of lust. But if ye would live soberly do not touch wine at all, lest ye sin in words of outrage, and in fightings and slanders, and transgressions of the commandments of God, and ye perish before your time. — Judah

Judah was the fourth son of Jacob and Leah. He was a giant of a man; both an athlete and a warrior. He was like a lion and earned his tribal totem by his heroic deeds. It is said that he could outrun a deer on the field.

Judah 1:1 The copy of the words of Judah, what things he spake to his sons before he died.

2 They gathered themselves together, therefore, and came to him, and he said to them: Hearken, my children, to Judah your father.

3 I was the fourth son born to my father Jacob; and Leah my mother named me Judah, saying, "I give thanks to the Lord, because He hath given me a fourth son also."

4 I was swift in my youth, and obedient to my father in everything.

5 And I honoured my mother and my mother's sister.

6 And it came to pass, when I became a man, that my father blessed me, saying, Thou shalt be a king, prospering in all things.

7 And the Lord showed me favour in all my works both in the field and in the house.

8 I know that I raced a hind, and caught it, and prepared the meat for my father, and he did eat.

9 And the roes I used to master in the chase, and overtake all that was in the plains.

That is pretty amazing. Any man who can outrun a deer, and catch it, is truly like a lion after prey. Such prowess tends to lack humility and Judah, and his family, have always struggled with pride.

10 A wild mare I overtook, and caught it and tamed it.

11 I slew a lion and plucked a kid out of its mouth.

12 I took a bear by its paw and hurled it down the cliff, and it was crushed.

13 I outran the wild boar, and seizing it as I ran, I tore it in sunder.

14 A leopard in Hebron leaped upon my dog, and I caught it by the tail, and hurled it on the rocks, and it was broken in twain

15 I found a wild ox feeding in the fields, and seizing it by the horns, and whirling it round and stunning it, I cast it from me and slew it.

16 And when the two kings of the Canaanites came sheathed in armour against our flocks, and much people with them, single handed I rushed upon the king of Hazor, and smote him on his legs and dragged him down, and so I slew him.

17 And the other, the king of Tappuah, as he sat upon his horse, I slew, and so I scattered all his people.

18 Achor, the king, a man of giant stature, I found, hurling javelins before and behind as he sat on horseback, and I took up a stone of sixty pounds weight, and hurled it and smote his horse, and killed it.

19 And I fought with this other for two hours; and I clave his shield in twain, and I chopped off his feet, and killed him.

20 And as I was stripping off his breastplate, behold nine men, his companions, began to fight with me,

21 And I wound my garment on my hand; and I slung stones at them, and killed four of them, and the rest fled.

It is from these great deeds that King David, though he was smaller than his brothers, knew that his tribe was a tribe of kings. Jesus, being their prize, was the King of the kings.

22 And Jacob my father slew Beelesath, king of all the kings, a giant in strength, twelve cubits high.

23 And fear fell upon them, and they ceased warring against us.

24 Therefore my father was free from anxiety in the wars when I was with my brethren.

A nice brag. Jacob could be a warrior when need be, although when Judah was with him, no one dared interfere. Later, when Judah was getting tough with Joseph in disguise in Egypt, it was Manasseh who dropped him with a punch.

25 For my father saw in a vision concerning me that an angel of might followed me everywhere, that I should not be overcome.

26 And in the south there came upon us a greater war than that in Shechem; and I joined in battle array with my brethren, and pursued a thousand men, and slew of them two hundred men and four kings.

27 And I went up upon the wall, and I slew four mighty men.

28 And so we captured Hazor, and took all the spoil.

29 And the next day we departed to Aretan, a city strong and walled and inaccessible, threatening us with death.

30 But I and Gad approached on the east side of the city, and Reuben and Levi on the west.

31 And they that were upon the wall, thinking that we were alone, were drawn down against us.

32 And so my brothers secretly climbed up the wall on both sides by stakes, and entered the city, while the men knew it not.

33 And we took it with the edge of the sword.

34 And as for those who had taken refuge in the tower, we set fire to the tower and took both it and them.

35 And as we were departing the men of Tappuah seized our spoil, and seeing this we fought with them.

36 And we slew them all and recovered our spoil.

37 And when I was at the waters of Kozeba, the men of Jobel came against us to battle.

38 And we fought with them and routed them; and their allies from Shiloh we slew, and we did not leave them power to come in against us.

39 And the men of Makir came upon us the fifth day, to seize our spoil; and we attacked them and overcame them in fierce battle: for there was a host of mighty men amongst them, and we slew them before they had gone up the ascent.

40 And when we came to their city their women rolled upon us stones from the brow of the hill on which the city stood.

41 And I and Simeon had ourselves behind the town, and seized upon the heights, and destroyed this city also.

42 And the next day it was told us that the king of the city of Gaash with a mighty host was coming against us.

43 I, therefore, and Dan feigned ourselves to be Amorites, and as allies went into their city.

44 And in the depth of night our brethren came and we opened to them the gates; and we destroyed all the men and their substance, and we took for a prey all that was theirs, and their three walls we cast down.

45 And we drew near to Thamna, where was all the substance of the hostile kings.

46 Then being insulted by them, I was therefore wroth, and rushed against them to the summit; and they kept slinging against me stones and darts.

47 And had not Dan my brother aided me, they would have slain me.

48 We came upon them, therefore, with wrath, and they all fled; and passing by another way, they fought my father, and he made peace with them.

49 And we did to them no hurt, and they became tributary to us, and we restored to them their spoil.

50 And I built Thamna, and my father built Pabael.

51 I was twenty years old when this war befell. And the Canaanites feared me and my brethren.

52 And I had much cattle, and I had for chief herdsman Iram the Adullamite.

53 And when I went to him I saw Parsaba, king of Adullam; and he spake unto us, and he made us a feast; and when I was heated in lust by wine he gave me his daughter Bathshua to wife.

54 She bare me Er, and Onan and Shelah; and two of them the Lord smote: for Shelah lived, and his children are ye [by Leverite Law].

Judah 2:1 And eighteen years my father abode in peace with his brother Esau, and his sons with us, after that we came from Mesopotamia, from Laban.

2 And when eighteen years were fulfilled, in the fortieth year of my life, Esau, the brother of my father, came upon us with a mighty and strong people.

3 And Jacob smote Esau with an arrow, and he was taken up wounded on Mount Seir, and as he went he died at Anoniram.

4 And we pursued after the sons of Esau.

This event is recounted also in the *Book of Jubilees*. Sadly, Jacob killed Esau in the end with an arrow. It must have been a terrible day for him.

5 Now they had a city with walls of iron and gates of brass; and we could not enter into it, and we encamped around, and besieged it.

6 And when they opened not to us in twenty days, I set up a ladder in the sight of all and with my shield upon my head I went up, sustaining the assault of stones, upwards of three talents weight; and I slew four of their mighty men.

7 And Reuben and Gad slew six others.

8 Then they asked from us terms of peace; and having taken counsel with our father, we received them as tributaries.

9 And they gave us five hundred cors of wheat, five hundred baths of oil, five hundred measures of wine, until the famine, when we went down into Egypt.

10 And after these things my son Er took to wife Tamar, from Mesopotamia, a daughter of Aram.

Aram was the son of the great Melchizedek, our Father Shem; the King and Priest of Salem. This is why the Lord wanted her married into Judah's line. It would also be King David's reason for claiming Jerusalem in the future. Tamar was a royal princess and Judah's Canaanite wife knew it and was jealous.

11 Now Er was wicked and didn't want Tamar because she was not of the land of Canaan and did not walk in their evil ways.

12 And on the third night an angel of the Lord smote him.

In other words, Er erred in having three chances to consummate their marriage but would not.

13 And he had not known her according to the evil craftiness of his mother, for he did not wish to have children by her.

14 In the days of the wedding feast I gave Onan to her in marriage; and he also in wickedness knew her not, though he spent with her a year.

15 And when I threatened him, he went in unto her, but he spilled the seed on the ground, according to the command of his mother, and would not give her a child, and he also died through wickedness too.

16 And I wished to give Shelah also to her, but his mother did not permit it; for she wrought evil against Tamar, because she was not the daughters of Canaan, as she also herself was.

17 And I knew that the race of the Canaanites was wicked, but the impulse of youth blinded my mind.

18 And when I saw her pouring out wine, owing to the intoxication of wine I was deceived, and took her although my father had not counselled it.

19 And while I was away she went and took for Shelah a wife from Canaan.

20 And when I knew what she had done, I cursed her in the anguish of my soul.

21 And she also died through her wickedness together with her sons.

22 And after these things, while Tamar was a widow, she heard after two years that I was going up, to shear my sheep, and adorned herself in bridal array, and sat in the city Enaim by the gate.

23 For it was a law of the Amorites, that she who was about to marry should sit in fornication seven days by the gate.

24 Therefore being drunk with wine, I did not recognize her; and her beauty deceived me, through the fashion of her adorning.

25 And I turned aside to her, and said: Let me go in unto thee.

26 And she said: What wilt thou give me? And I gave her my staff, and my girdle, and the diadem of my kingdom in pledge.

27 And I went in unto her, and she conceived.

28 And not knowing what I had done, I wished to slay her; but she privily sent my pledges, and put me to shame.

29 And when I called her, I heard also the secret words which I spoke when lying with her in my drunkenness; and I could not slay her, because it was from the Lord.

30 For I said, Lest haply she did it in subtlety, having received the pledge from another woman.

31 But I came not again near her while I lived, because I had done this abomination in all Israel.

32 Moreover, they who were in the city said there was no harlot in the gate, because she came from another place, and sat for a while in the gate.

33 And I thought that no one knew that I had gone in to her.

34 And after this we came into Egypt to Joseph, because of the famine.

35 And I was forty and six years old, and seventy and three years lived I in Egypt.

Judah decries wine and lust. They are the twin evils. Men who are drunk or high are proud, stupid, and sinful in the end.

Judah 3:1 And now I command you, my children, hearken to Judah your father, and keep my sayings to perform all the ordinances of the Lord, and to obey the commands of God.

2 And walk not after your lusts, nor in the imaginations of your thoughts in haughtiness of heart; and glory not in the deeds and strength of your youth, for this also is evil in the eyes of the Lord.

3 Since I also gloried that in wars no comely woman's face ever enticed me, and reproved Reuben my brother concerning Bilhah, the wife of my father, the

spirits of jealousy and of fornication arrayed themselves against me, until I lay with Bathshua the Canaanite, and Tamar, who was espoused to my sons.

4 For I said to my father-in-law: I will take counsel with my father, and see if he will allow me to take thy Canaanite daughter.

5 And he was unwilling to speak to my father but he showed me a boundless store of gold in his daughter's behalf; for he was a king.

6 And he adorned her with gold and pearls, and caused her to pour out wine for us at the feast with the beauty of women.

7 And the wine turned aside my eyes, and pleasure blinded my heart.

8 And I became enamoured of and I lay with her, and transgressed the commandment of the Lord and the commandment of my fathers, and I took her to wife.

9 And the Lord rewarded me according to the imagination of my heart, inasmuch as I had no joy in her children.

10 And now, my children, I say unto you, be not drunk with wine; for wine turneth the mind away from, the truth, and inspires the passion of lust, and leadeth the eyes into error.

11 For the spirit of fornication hath wine as a minister to give pleasure to the mind; for these two also take away the mind of man.

12 For if a man drink wine to drunkenness, it disturbeth the mind with filthy thoughts leading to fornication, and heateth the body to carnal union; and if the occasion of the lust be present, he worketh the sin, and is not ashamed.

13 Such is the inebriated man, my children; for he who is drunken reverenceth no man.

14 For, lo, it made me also to err, so that I was not ashamed of the multitude in the city, in that before the eyes of all I turned aside unto Tamar, and I wrought a great sin, and I uncovered the covering of my sons' shame.

15 After I had drunk wine I reverenced not the commandment of God, and I took a woman of Canaan to wife.

16 For much discretion needeth the man who drinketh wine, my children; and herein is discretion in drinking wine, a man may drink so long as he preserveth modesty.

17 But if he go beyond this limit the spirit of deceit attacketh his mind, and it maketh the drunkard to talk filthily, and to transgress and not to be ashamed, but even to glory in his shame, and to account himself honourable.

18 He that committeth fornication is not aware when he suffers loss, and is not ashamed when put to dishonour.

19 For even though a man be a king and commit fornication, he is stripped of his kingship by becoming the slave of fornication, as I myself also suffered.

20 For I gave my staff, that is, the stay of my tribe; and my girdle, that is, my power; and my diadem, that is, the glory of my kingdom.

21 And indeed I repented of these things; wine and flesh I eat not until my old age, nor did I behold any joy.

22 And the angel of God showed me that for ever do women bear rule over king and beggar alike.

23 And from the king they take away his glory, and from the valiant man his might, and from the beggar even that little which is the stay of his poverty.

This was said for King David and Solomon's sake and they would have read these words, but they didn't listen to them in the day of their temptation.

24 Observe, therefore, my children, the right limit in wine; for there are in it four evil spirits - -of lust, of hot desire, of profligacy, of filthy lucre.

25 If ye drink wine in gladness, be ye modest in the fear of God.

26 For if in your gladness the fear of God departeth, then drunkenness ariseth and shamelessness stealeth in.

27 But if ye would live soberly do not touch wine at all, lest ye sin in words of outrage, and in fightings and slanders, and transgressions of the commandments of God, and ye perish before your time.

28 Moreover, wine can betray your oath concerning the mysteries of God and secrets of your fellowmen, even as I also revealed the endowment of God and the mysteries of Jacob my father to the Canaanite woman Bathshua, which God bade me not to reveal.

29 And wine is a cause both of war and confusion.

30 And now, I command you, my children, not to love money, nor to gaze upon the beauty of women; because for the sake of money and beauty I was led astray to Bathshua the Canaanite.

31 For I know that because of these two things shall my tribe fall into wickedness.

32 For even wise men among my sons shall they mar, and shall cause the kingdom of Judah to be diminished, which the Lord gave me because of my obedience to my father.

33 For I never caused grief to Jacob, my father; for all things whatsoever he commanded I did.

This is ultimately why Judah prospered and gained the right to the Messiah. Like the Lord Jesus Christ, Judah always obeyed the will of his Father when he knew it. In this he was a type of Jesus and the Father.

34 And Isaac, the father of my father, blessed me to be king in Israel, and Jacob further blessed me in like manner.

35 And I know that from me shall the kingdom be established.

36 And I know what evils ye will do in the last days.

37 Beware, therefore, my children, of fornication, and the love of money, and hearken to Judah your father.

38 For these things withdraw you from the law of God, and blind the inclination of the soul, and teach arrogance, and suffer not a man to have compassion upon his neighbour.

39 They rob his soul of all goodness, and oppress him with toils and troubles, and drive away sleep from him, and devour his flesh.

40 And he hindereth the sacrifices of God; and he remembereth not the blessing of God, he hearkeneth not to a prophet when he speaketh, and resenteth the words of godliness.

41 For he is a slave to two contrary passions, and cannot obey God, because they have blinded his soul, and he walketh in darkness as though it be day.

42 My children, the love of money leadeth to idolatry; because, when led astray through money, men name as gods those who are not gods, and it causeth him who hath it to fall into madness.

43 For the sake of money I lost my children, and had not my repentance, and my humiliation, and the prayers of my father been accepted, I should have died childless.

44 But the God of my fathers had mercy on me, because I did it in ignorance.

45 And the prince of deceit blinded me, and I sinned as a man and as flesh, being corrupted through sins; and I learnt my own weakness while thinking myself invincible.

46 Know, therefore, my children, that two spirits wait upon man the spirit of truth and the spirit of deceit.

47 And in the midst is the spirit of understanding of the mind, to which it belongeth to turn whithersoever it will.

48 And the works of truth and the works of deceit are written upon the hearts of men, and each one of them the Lord knoweth.

49 And there is no time at which the works of men can be hid; for on the heart itself have they been written down before the Lord.

50 And the spirit of truth testifieth all things, and accuseth all; and the sinner is burnt up by his own heart, and cannot raise his face to the judge.

Judah 4:1 And now, my children, I command you, love Levi, that ye may abide, and exalt not yourselves against him, lest ye be utterly destroyed.

2 For to me the Lord gave the kingdom, and to him the priesthood, and He set the kingdom beneath the priesthood.

3 To me He gave the things upon the earth; to him the things in the heavens.

4 As the heaven is higher than the earth, so is the priesthood of God higher than the earthly kingdom, unless it falls away through sin from the Lord and is dominated by the earthly kingdom.

A very interesting understanding and the oldest, clearly spelled out need to separate church and state.

5 For the angel of the Lord said unto me: "The Lord chose him rather than thee, to draw near to Him, and to eat of His table and to offer Him the first-fruits of the choice things of the sons of Israel; but thou shalt be king of Jacob."

6 And thou shalt be amongst them as the sea.

7 For as, on the sea, just and unjust are tossed about, some taken into captivity while some are enriched, so also shall every race of men be in thee: some shall be impoverished, being taken captive, and others grow rich by plundering the possessions of others.

8 For the kings shall be as sea-monsters.

9 They shall swallow men like fishes: the sons and daughters of freemen shall they enslave; houses, lands, flocks, money shall they plunder:

10 And with the flesh of many shall they wrongfully feed the ravens and the cranes; and they shall advance in evil in covetousness uplifted, and there shall be false prophets like tempest, and they shall persecute all righteous men.

Ravens and Cranes are unclean birds in Israeli thinking. Also ravens seek death and follow their own way. When Noah released a raven from the ark, it would not come back to him.

11 And the Lord shall bring upon them divisions one against another.

12 And there shall be continual wars in Israel; and among men of another race shall my kingdom be brought to an end, until the salvation of Israel shall come.

These unclean ones, like ravens and cranes, would be the children of Esau and Ishmael, who today make up both the houses of Rome and Arabia.

13 Until the appearing of the God of righteousness, that Jacob, and all the Nations may rest in peace.

14 And He shall guard the might of my kingdom for ever; for the Lord swore to me with an oath that He would not destroy the kingdom from my seed for ever.

15 Now I have much grief, my children, because of your lewdness and witchcrafts, and idolatries which ye shall practice against the kingdom, following them that have familiar spirits, diviners, and demons of error.

16 Ye shall make your daughters singing girls and harlots, and ye shall mingle in the abominations of the Gentiles.

17 For which things' sake the Lord shall bring upon you famine and pestilence, death and the sword, beleaguering by enemies, and revilings of friends, the slaughter of children, the rape of wives, the plundering of possessions, the

burning of the temple of God, the laying waste of the land, and the enslavement of yourselves among the Gentiles.

18 And they shall make some of you eunuchs for their wives.

Daniel and likely Shadrach, Meshach, and Abednego, all princes of Judah were made into eunuchs at the whim of Nebuchadnezzar.

Next comes one the clearest prophecies of the Messiah Ben Judah – Jesus the Christ – that has survived to us from antiquity:

19 Until the Lord visit you, when with perfect heart ye repent and walk in all His commandments, and He bring you up from captivity among the Gentiles.

20 And after these things shall a star arise to you from Jacob in peace,

21 And a man shall arise from my seed, like the sun of righteousness,

22 Walking with the sons of men in meekness and righteousness;

23 And no sin shall be found in him.

24 And the heavens shall be opened unto him, to pour out the spirit, even the blessing of the Holy Father; and He shall pour out the spirit of grace upon you;

25 And ye shall be unto Him sons in truth, and ye shall walk in His commandments first and last.

26 Then shall the scepter of my kingdom shine forth; and from your root shall arise a stem; and from it shall grow a rod of righteousness to the Gentiles, to judge and to save all that call upon the Lord.

27 And after these things shall Abraham and Isaac and Jacob arise unto life; and I and my brethren shall be chiefs of the tribes of Israel:

28 Levi first, I the second, Joseph third, Benjamin fourth, Simeon fifth, Issachar sixth, and so all in order.

29 And the Lord blessed Levi, and the Angel of the Presence, me; the powers of glory, Simeon; the heaven, Reuben; the earth, Issachar; the sea, Zebulun; the mountains, Joseph; the tabernacle, Benjamin; the luminaries, Dan; Eden, Naphtali; the sun, Gad; the moon, Asher.

30 And ye shall be the people of the Lord, and have one tongue; and there shall be there no spirit of deceit of Beliar, for he shall be cast into the fire for ever.

31 And they who have died in grief shall arise in joy, and they who were poor for the Lord's sake shall be made rich, and they who are put to death for the Lord's sake shall awake to life.

32 And the harts of Jacob shall run in joyfulness, and the eagles of Israel shall fly in gladness; and all the people shall glorify the Lord for ever.

33 Observe, therefore, my children, all the law of the Lord, for there is hope for all them who hold fast unto, His ways.

34 And he said to them: Behold, I die before your eyes this day, a hundred and nineteen years old.

35 Let no one bury me in costly apparel, nor tear open my bowels [and embalm me], for this shall they who are kings do; only carry me up to Hebron with you.

36 And Judah, when he had said these things, fell asleep; and his sons did according to all whatsoever he commanded them, and they buried him in Hebron, with his fathers.

Genesis 46:12 And the sons of Judah; Er, and Onan, and Shelah, [by Bathsua] and Pharez, and Zerah [by Tamar]: but Er and Onan died in the land of Canaan. And the sons of Pharez were Hezron and Hamul.

LATTER-DAY LESSONS FROM FATHER JUDAH

Judah's parting words do much to clarify the Lord's rationale for choosing him as the father of the kings and as patriarch of the Messiah's tribe. The accounts of Judah from the Bible alone, leave much to be desired. There he is seen as a money monger, an adulator, and a cad. Hearing his own rationale for his actions shows us the nature of his heart. In many ways he was a man trying to play catch up from one bad decision. His choices had put the Lord in a difficult position as well. Since the Messiah was to come through Judah, the fact that he had married a Canaanite was a real problem. He tried to right the wrong by making a match for his eldest with one of Shem's daughters, but even in that he was erring before the Lord.

For the children of Canaan had been cursed by Father Noah and so it would not have been possible for the Messiah to have come through Judah's sons by Bathshua.[19] Here we learn that Tamar was the granddaughter of Melchizedek (or Shem) whose legal capital was Jerusalem. Thus it all makes sense.

While we all have a way of justifying our actions and thinking processes when given the chance to explain ourselves, Judah's record really does read like a highly gifted man who didn't really need anyone until he learned that he did. In his youth, he was strong and handsome, rich and admired. He embraced all of it and really only stumbled when he allowed wine, money, and women to overcome his sensibilities. The wonderful thing about Judah's life story is the great patience of the Lord. He knew that Judah would grow up and become one of the great patriarchs of humanity. Judah never abandoned the Lord, he only abandoned his good judgement. In that is the lesson, whatever we are or are not, whatever it is that we do or have done, if we will cling to the Lord and not forsake him, there is hope; for the Lord is mighty to save. Judah shows us that immature, mortal humanity will always put God in this conundrum. Men are made in the image of the gods. Enlightened by the spirit of truth, we are the very children of the highest. Combined with joy of our creation, and the truth that "no man hateth his own flesh," we are caught with God in the need to balance all of this grandeur with a wise and sober heart. In the end this is the gift of the Father, the lessons of mortality. Our ability to return with these lessons home to the throne, is the gift of Jesus the Son. Judah got it in the end. God's hope is that you will too.

Judah's own account of the sale of Joseph differs from the Sunday School jokes about "Jews and Money" which we hear every time we study the story from *Genesis*. Judah here insists that selling Joseph was the only way to save him; which actually may have been true. Both Dan and Simeon would later say that they fully intended to murder Joseph and that at some point it would have happened. Judah furthers the future sign of the Messiah that salvation would come through the favored son sold into slavery for a price. When Reuben fell and Simeon proved himself unworthy, and with Levi becoming the tithe of the family, (the priestly house), the heir in terms of Leah's family fell on Judah.

Here we also get a clue as to the Lord's pre-clearing of the land at the hands of Israel and his sons. These were events that we thought did not happened until Joshua. We also get a better understanding of the famine that was coming on the land and why Israel needed to be safely ensconced in Egypt. The famine that struck the planet caused much greater upheavals and wars between cultures and city-states than we understand from the *Bible* text alone. In a very real and serious way, these restored books help us understand that the famine in the days of Jacob, the gathering of Israel to the deserts of Egypt for a season, there to be protected and mentored by one of the sons, lost and separated from the family, the growing in strength despite bondage and the eventual return to honor in the holy land, was a replaying of the Lord's plan for the last days. It is one great sign in which we are the major players. We will discuss this in more detail when we study Joseph's testimony. For now, it is important to know that while latter-day Joseph is busily preparing the deserts of Utah for the return of the lost family, Judah is gathering home to Jerusalem. When the Lord calls an end to the missionary labors, the testimony of nature will begin. During this time, the Lord will return the Lost Ten Tribes to us. When they come, they will find temples, homes, lands, fields and food ready for them in the arms of Joseph in the mountains.[20]

With all this new information from Judah, Father Israel's blessing on his head makes a lot more sense.

Genesis 49: 8 Judah, thou art he whom thy brethren shall praise: thy hand shall be in the neck of thine enemies; thy father's children shall bow down before thee.

9 Judah is a lion's whelp: from the prey, my son, thou art gone up: he stooped down, he couched as a lion, and as an old lion; who shall rouse him up?

10 The sceptre shall not depart from Judah, nor a lawgiver from between his feet, until Shiloh come; and unto him shall the gathering of the people be.

Shiloh in Hebrew means *he whose right it is* meaning that Judah's right to rule would continue with the Tribe of Judah until the Messiah appeared. What should have been a sign to the people was eventually misunderstood. In the year 30 A.D., Rome removed the Jewish sovereignty, effectively taking away their independence. It most closely manifested itself in their loss of the power of execution. When the rabbis and powerful Jews realized it, they went into the streets and ripped their garments in sorrow that the Promises of God had failed. What they should have done instead was search their ranks for the fulfillment of the sign that somewhere "he whose right it was to rule Israel" was walking among them. Christians know that at this same time, John the Levitical High Priest had chosen the very Lamb! Jesus of Nazareth was openly preaching the Kingdom of Heaven among the people. Shiloh had come!

Genesis 49:11 Binding his foal unto the vine, and his ass's colt unto the choice vine; he washed his garments in wine, and his clothes in the blood of grapes:

The Rabbis say that this is both a slap and a promise of a second Messiah, not the greater Messiah Son of Judah, but the Restoring Messiah the son of Joseph. The imagery is deeply eastern. The foal is Judah but the vine is Joseph. The first Messiah would walk the wine press alone but the bounty of the wine would be the fruitfulness of Joseph, whose totem was the vine and the bountiful harvest.

Genesis 49:12 His eyes shall be red with wine, and his teeth white with milk.

This is a statement of abundance. Moses, as High Priest of the nation, would add this prophetic plea:

Deuteronomy 33:7 Hear, Lord, the voice of Judah, and bring him unto his people: let his hands be sufficient for him; and be thou an help to him from his enemies.

Chapter Five

Issachar

The single-minded man waiteth only for the will of God. — Issachar

Issachar was the fifth son of Jacob and Leah. He was one of the children of hire for Reuben's mandrakes. He appeals for simplicity in life and for having one's eye on the glory of God alone. He was a good and righteous man.

Issachar 1:1 The copy of the words of Issachar.

2 For he called his sons and said to them: Hearken, my children, to Issachar your father; give ear to the words of him who is beloved of the Lord.

3 I was born the fifth son to Jacob *and* Leah, by way of hire for the mandrakes.

4 For Reuben my brother brought in mandrakes from the field, and Rachel met him and took them.

The implication is that Reuben meant them to be a gift for his mother. He was 13 years old at the time.

5 And Reuben wept, and at his voice Leah my mother came forth.

6 Now these mandrakes were sweet-smelling apples which were produced in the land of Haran below a ravine of water.

7 And Rachel said: "I will not give them to thee, but they shall be to me instead of children.

8 For the Lord hath despised me, and I have not borne children to Jacob."

This shows how bitter the situation had become in the family over children.

9 Now there were two apples; and Leah said to Rachel: "Isn't it enough that you have taken my husband away from me at night? Would you also have my son's gift to his mother?"

10 And Rachel said to her: "Thou shalt have Jacob this night for the mandrakes of thy son."

11 And Leah said to her: "Jacob is already mine, for I am the wife of his youth."

In other words, *"I am the first wife, you know."*

12 But Rachel said: "Boast not, and vaunt not thyself; for he espoused me before thee, and for my sake he served our father fourteen years.

13 And had not craft increased on the earth and the wickedness of men prospered, thou wouldst not now see the face of Jacob.

Only by deceit was her reply. He bought me twice!

14 For thou art not his wife, only in deceit did you take him from me.

15 And my father deceived me, and removed me on that night, and did not suffer Jacob to see me; for had I been there, this would not have happened to him.

This is an interesting clue to these marriage events. It makes a lot of sense. Of course Rachel would have stopped her father's deception if she could have. She loved Jacob and they wanted to be together. I suspect they would have eloped had they known what Laban had it store for them.

16 Nevertheless, for the mandrakes I am hiring Jacob to thee for one night."

17 And Jacob knew Leah, and she conceived and bare me, and on account of the hire I was called Issachar.

This also makes sense. Jacob used Leah for children but was sleeping in pleasure with Rachel. When Leah's son found his mother a present of sweet mandrakes, Rachel was jealous that she didn't have a son to bring her some. She thereby took what was to be Leah's gift. Leah said to her, "Fine, but then I get Jacob tonight." Rachel gave in and the Lord blessed Leah yet again with another son.

18 Then appeared to Jacob an angel of the Lord, saying: "Two children shall Rachel bear, inasmuch as she hath refused company with her husband, and hath chosen sexual self-restraint."

19 And had not Leah my mother paid the two apples for the sake of his company, she would have borne eight sons; for this reason she bare six, and Rachel bare the two: for on account of the mandrakes the Lord visited her.[21]

Rachel also seems to have believed this as is born out in other texts. Although she was selfish, justifiably hurt, and angry about the mandrakes, she was willing to share Jacob and the Lord blessed her for it. The message is clear. The Lord expects a man to love his wife and a wife to love her husband. As Lord, He has promised to take all and any of us to His bosom who will legally come. He will love even the least lovely of us. We are to do the same in this life. Love those in our charge and stewardship. We are to be charitable and try to see the bigger picture.

20 For the Lord knew that for the sake of children Rachel wished to have Jacob then, and not just for lust or pleasure.

21 For on the morrow also she again gave up Jacob in fasting and sacrifice.

22 Because of the mandrake offering, therefore, the Lord hearkened to Rachel.

23 For though she desired them, she ate them not, but offered them as a sacrifice in the house of the Lord, presenting them to the rightful priest of the Most High who was presiding at that time.

So, according to Issachar, Rachel made the mandrakes an offering to the Lord. I am sure that she also made promises to Him at that time as well. What she promised is not known, but we can imply that it had to do with sharing Jacob, and loving Leah, and her children with a better heart.[22]

24 When, therefore, I grew up, my children, I walked in uprightness of heart, and I became a husbandman for my father and my brethren, and I brought in fruits from the field according to their season.

25 And my father blessed me, for he saw that I walked in truthfulness before him.

Most of Jacob's sons were shepherds, but Issachar took over the family orchards and fields. We know from other sources that the older boys, who were managing their father's substantial herds, were also selling off some of them for themselves and sleeping around with local women. Jacob knew of some of this but wasn't certain how to stop it. Issachar seems to have escaped his brother's sins by farming closer to home and placing himself under his father's rule.

26 And I was not a busybody in my doings, nor envious and malicious against my neighbour.

27 I never slandered any one, nor did I censure the life of any man, walking as I did in singleness of eye.

28 Therefore, when I was thirty-five years old, I took to myself a wife, for my labour wore away my strength, and I never thought upon pleasure with women; but owing to my toil, sleep overcame me.

29 And my father always rejoiced in my obedience, because I offered through the priest to the Lord all first-fruits; then to my father also.

30 And the Lord increased ten thousandfold His benefits in my hands; and also Jacob, my father, knew that God aided my singleness.

Issachar worked hard and didn't have a lot of energy left over for his libido. He is likely comparing this to Reuben and Judah who struggled in this area extensively.

31 For on all the poor and oppressed I bestowed the good things of the earth in the singleness of my heart.

32 And now, hearken to me, my children, and walk in singleness of your heart, for I have seen in it all that is well-pleasing to the Lord.

33 The single-minded man coveteth not gold, he overreacheth not his neighbour, he longeth not after manifold dainties, he delighteth not in varied apparel.

34 He doth not desire to live a long life, but only waiteth for the will of God.[23]

35 And the spirits of deceit have no power against him, for he looketh not on the beauty of women, lest he should pollute his mind with corruption.

36 There is no envy in his thoughts, no malicious person maketh his soul to pine away, nor worry with insatiable desire in his mind.

37 For he walketh in singleness of soul, and beholdeth all things in uprightness of heart, shunning eyes made evil through the error of the world, lest he should see the perversion of any of the commandments of the Lord.

38 Keep, therefore, my children, the law of God, and get singleness, and walk in guilelessness, not playing the busybody with the business of your neighbour, but love the Lord and your neighbour, have compassion on the poor and weak.

39 Bow down your back unto husbandry, and toil in labours in all manner of husbandry, offering gifts to the Lord with thanksgiving.

In other words: *Do not see the labour forced upon man as a curse but see it as a blessing and rejoice that God has made us to till the ground and reap the good that we sow.*

40 For with the first-fruits of the earth will the Lord bless you, even as He blessed all the saints from Abel even until now.

This explains the eastern understanding of *First Fruits*. A husbandman tilling the ground can't be sure that his efforts will succeed but he does so out of faith that God will bless him. When the first fruits of labour appear it is proof of the promise. By giving this to the Lord you are acknowledging that it was He who taught you to live by faith by giving you the command that led to your blessing. The Lord's sacrifice was the first fruit to the Father in just the same way. It is a double symbol.

41 For no other portion is given to you than of the fatness of the earth, whose fruits are raised by toil.

42 For our father Jacob blessed me with blessings of the earth and of first-fruits.

43 And Levi and Judah were glorified by the Lord even among the sons of Jacob; for the Lord gave them an inheritance, and to Levi He gave the priesthood, and to Judah the kingdom.

44 And do ye therefore obey them, and walk in the singleness of your father; for unto Gad hath it been given to destroy the troops that are coming upon Israel.

Issachar 2:1 Know ye therefore, my children, that in the last times your sons will forsake singleness, and will cleave unto insatiable desire.

Hence this patriarch's trying to warn his sons to be single minded in serving the Lord.

2 And leaving guilelessness, will draw near to malice; and forsaking the commandments of the Lord, they will cleave unto Beliar.

3 And leaving husbandry, they will follow after their own wicked devices, and they shall be dispersed among the Gentiles, and shall serve their enemies.

4 And do you therefore give these commands to your children, that, if they sin, they may the more quickly return to the Lord; for He is merciful, and will deliver them, even to bring them back into their land.

5 Behold, therefore, as ye see, I am a hundred and twenty-six years old and am not conscious of committing any sin.

6 Except my wife I have not known any woman. I never committed fornication by the uplifting of my eyes.

7 I drank not wine, to be led astray thereby;

8 I coveted not any desirable thing that was my neighbour's.

9 Guile arose not in my heart;

10 A lie passed not through my lips.

11 If any man were in distress I joined my sighs with his,

12 And I shared my bread with the poor.

13 I wrought godliness, all my days I kept truth.

14 I loved the Lord; likewise also every man with all my heart.

15 So do you also these things, my children, and every spirit of Beliar shall flee from you, and no deed of wicked men shall rule over you;

16 And every wild beast shall ye subdue, since you have with you the God of heaven and earth and walk with men in singleness of heart.

17 And having said these things, he commanded his sons that they should carry him up to Hebron, and bury him there in the cave with his fathers.

18 And he stretched out his feet and died, at a good old age; with every limb sound, and with strength unabated, he slept the eternal sleep.

Genesis 46:13 And the sons of Issachar; Tola, and Phuvah, and Job [24], and Shimron.

LATTER-DAY LESSONS FROM FATHER ISSACHAR

As a son of Ephraim, the greatest gift of uncle Issachar is his witness of our mother Rachel. She, like Jacob, was wronged by her father and Leah. Place yourself in Jacob and Rachel's shoes a moment. They dearly loved each other. Laban made a contract with Jacob for Rachel to which Rachel agreed. He threw a large party, got Jacob wasted, whisked Rachel away on a lie and got Jacob to consummate a wedding with Leah. When Rachel came back home, she discovered that her father was a lying puke and that the man she loved had just impregnated her sister. It is a terrible story when you really stop and think about it.

When it comes to affairs of the heart, men and women have committed murder over less than what Laban did to Jacob! Issachar shows us that it was Rachel's humble supplication to the Lord that brought about the blessing in the end. While I tremble to besmirch the mother of my tribe, and the love of Father Israel, from other ancient records we learn that Rachel may have struggled with idol worship at first, while Leah seems to have embraced Jacob's God early. This is based on educated speculation and so we cannot say with certainty but the clues are there in the texts.

A god-fearing mother, more often than a god-fearing father, sets the tone in a home. Children learn to honor the patriarchal priesthood order by watching their mothers honor it. Since the Lord intended great things for the house of Israel (and note that home is feminine in eastern thinking), He needed mothers 100% committed to the plan. Part member families can attest that it is particularly hard on children when the mom doesn't believe. In the end, this was the deepest pain of Judah's heart. When he married a woman who was unwilling and unworthy to raise his princes in the gospel, nothing but pain and sadness prevailed. Judah's sons chose their mother's religion and counsel over their fathers. The Lord slew them all (and their mother) in the end. The Lord takes covenants extremely seriously and if promises have been made to you and yours, which will affect the greater plan, you would be wise to keep up your end of the covenant.

Zion is symbolically female and when mom isn't nurturing her chicks beneath the canopy of Zion, there is no glue to bind the family together. It is illustrative to note that as soon as Rachel made sacrifice to the God of Abraham, Isaac and her Husband, the Lord heard her. While it is only my suspicion, I think that Rachel covenanted with the Lord to raise her children to the God of Israel as well as other promises which may have put her in similar stead to mothers like Hannah.

Issachar teaches that by throwing himself into his duty; working by the sweat of his brow to provide for himself and others he found joy, purpose, and blessing. In short he fulfilled the measure of his creation, which in the parlance of heaven is the definition of Celestialization. Issachar was a good man and as such lived a life of less sorrow due to his own actions. His greatest sorrow came from watching the pain that others in the family caused him, his father, his mother and the entire household. His father blessed him thus:

Genesis 49:14 Issachar is a strong ass couching down between two burdens:

15 And he saw that rest was good, and the land that it was pleasant; and bowed his shoulder to bear, and became a servant unto tribute.

Moses said: "Rejoice in thy tents, Issachar." If you can't be the boss but must work under tribute for a season, you can at least take joy in your home and your family. How many men in this world understand that truth. Until the Great Beast is finally crushed beneath the foot of the Messiah, all of us end up rendering lucre to Caesar.

Chapter Six

Zebulun

*He that shareth with his neighbour
receiveth manifold more from the Lord.* — *Zebulun*

Zebulun was the sixth son of Jacob and Leah. He was an inventor and a philanthropist. We learn from Zebulun how the sin of omission can be as painful to bare in retrospect as the sin of commission, but he can speak for himself:

Zebulun 1:1 The copy of the words of Zebulun, which he enjoined on his sons before he died in the hundred and fourteenth year of his life, thirty-two years after the death of Joseph.

2 And he said to them: Hearken to me, ye sons of Zebulun attend to the words of your father.

3 I, Zebulun, was born a good gift to my parents.

4 For when I was born my father was increased very exceedingly, both in flocks and herds, when with the streaked rods he had his portion.

Jacob had discovered that flock, like people, respond to the erotic. The stakes before the flocks were meant to arouse the animals into mating. We learn from the scriptures that it worked.

5 I am not conscious that I have sinned all my days, save in thought.

6 Nor yet do I remember that I have done any iniquity, except the sin of ignorance which I committed against Joseph; for I covenanted with my brethren not to tell my father what had been done.

7 But I wept in secret many days on account of Joseph, for I feared my brethren, because they had all agreed that if any one should declare the secret, he should be slain.

8 But when they wished to kill him, I adjured them much with tears not to be guilty of this sin.

Zebulun spoke mercy and spared Joseph's life but he would not stand up and stop them from the act of selling him. What is really wonderful, and tragic, is that he preserved for us Joseph's last words at the time of their murderous plot. It does beg the question of each of us, *are we ashamed of Christ's name in our day?*

9 For Simeon and Gad came against Joseph to kill him, and he said unto them with tears: "Pity me, my brethren, have mercy upon the bowels of Jacob our father: lay not upon me your hands to shed innocent blood, for I have not sinned against you.

10 And if indeed I have sinned, with chastening chastise me, my brethren, but lay not upon me your hand, for the sake of Jacob our father."

11 And as he spoke these words, wailing as he did so, I was unable to bear his lamentations, and began to weep, and my liver was poured out, and all the substance of my bowels was loosened.

12 And I wept with Joseph and my heart sounded, and the joints of my body trembled, and I was not able to stand.

13 And when Joseph saw me weeping with him, and them coming against him to slay him, he fled behind me, beseeching them.

Wow! Can you see it?

14 But meanwhile Reuben arose and said: "Come, my brethren, let us not slay him, but let us cast him into one of these dry pits, which our fathers digged and found no water."

Zebulun has an interesting take on this from the perspective of his maturity.

15 For for this cause the Lord forbade that water should rise up in them in order that Joseph should be preserved.

16 And they did so, until they sold him to the Ishmaelites.

17 For in his price I had no share, my children.

18 But Simeon and Gad and six other of our brethren took the price of Joseph, and bought sandals for themselves, and their wives, and their children, saying:

19 "We will not eat of it, for it is the price of our brother's blood, but we will assuredly tread it under foot, because he said that he would be king over us, and so let us see what will become of his dreams."

20 *Therefore it is written in the writing of the law of Moses, that whosoever will not raise up seed to his brother, his sandal should be unloosed, and they should spit in his face.*

Verses 20-25 consist of commentary added by a later Rabbi. If our Rabbinical guide is correct, the very interesting custom of removing one's shoe in shame (which even occurs in modern temples) is a sign of the brother whose blood was sold for another. Interesting, but the unknown Rabbi-editor added a bit more:

21 *And the brethren of Joseph wished not that their brother should live, and the Lord loosed from them the sandal which they wore against Joseph their brother.*

22 *For when they came into Egypt they were unloosed by the servants of Joseph outside the gate, and so they made obeisance to Joseph after the fashion of King Pharaoh.*

23 *And not only did they make obeisance to him, but were spit upon also, falling down before him forthwith, and so they were put to shame before the Egyptians.*

24 *For after this the Egyptians heard all the evils that they had done to Joseph.*

25 *And how after he was sold his brothers sat down to eat and drink.*

Zebulun continues:

26 But I, through pity for Joseph, did not eat, but watched the pit, since Judah feared lest Simeon, Dan, and Gad should rush off and slay him.[25]

27 But when they saw that I did not eat, they set me to watch him, till he was sold to the Ishmaelites.

Zebulun also preserves for us Reuben's words when he discovered what they had done:

28 And when Reuben came and heard that while he was away Joseph had been sold, he rent his garments, and mourning, said:

29 "How shall I look on the face of my father Jacob? And he took the money and ran after the merchants but as he failed to find them he returned grieving."

30 But the merchants had left the broad road and marched through the Troglodytes by a short cut.

31 But Reuben was grieved, and ate no food that day.

32 Dan therefore came to him and said: "Weep not, neither grieve; for we have found what we can say to our father Jacob.

33 Let us slay a kid of the goats, and dip in it the coat of Joseph; and let us send it to Jacob, saying: 'Know, is this the coat of thy son?'"

34 And they did so. For they stripped off from Joseph his coat when they were selling him, and put upon him the garment of a slave.

35 Now Simeon took the coat, and would not give it up, for he wished to rend it with his sword, as he was angry that Joseph lived and that he had not slain him.

36 Then we all rose up and said unto him: "If thou givest not up the coat, we will say to our father that thou alone didst this evil thing in Israel."

What a conspiracy! One of the reasons that I believe this book to be authentic is the very interesting juxtaposition by each brother of what they reveal and what they leave out. It is filled with human nature and drama and very credible.

37 And so he gave it unto them, and they did even as Dan had said.

Zebulun 2:1 And now children, I command you to keep the commands of the Lord, and to show mercy to your neighbours, and to have compassion towards all, not towards men only, but also towards beasts.

2 For the sake of all these things the Lord blessed me, and when all my brethren were sick, I escaped without sickness, for the Lord knoweth the purposes of each.

3 Have, therefore, compassion in your hearts, my children, because even as a man doeth to his neighbour, even so also will the Lord do to him.

4 For the sons of my brethren were sickening and were dying on account of Joseph, because they showed not mercy in their hearts; but my sons were preserved without sickness, as ye know.

Zebulun will next give us some insight into the great famine and world that they were living in while Joseph was in Egypt:

5 And when I was in the land of Canaan, by the sea-coast, I made a catch of fish for Jacob my father; and when many were choked in the sea, I continued unhurt.

6 I was the first to make a boat to sail upon the sea, for the Lord gave me understanding and wisdom therein.

7 And I let down a rudder behind it, and I stretched a sail upon another upright piece of wood in the midst.

8 And I sailed therein along the shores, catching fish for the house of my father until we came to Egypt.

This explains Israel's strange blessing on Zebulun's head:

Genesis 49:13 Zebulun shall dwell at the haven of the sea; and he shall be for an haven of ships; and his border shall be unto Zidon.

A beautiful reminder of Zebulun's gift of food in famine.

9 And through compassion I shared my catch with every stranger.

10 And if a man were a stranger, or sick, or aged, I boiled the fish, and dressed them well, and offered them to all men, as every man had need, grieving with and having compassion upon them.

11 Wherefore also the Lord satisfied me with abundance of fish when catching fish; for he that shareth with his neighbour receiveth manifold more from the Lord.

12 For five years I caught fish and gave thereof to every man whom I saw, and sufficed for all the house of my father.

13 And in the summer I caught fish, and in the winter I kept sheep with my brethren.

14 Now I will declare unto you what I did.

15 I saw a man in distress through nakedness in wintertime, and had compassion upon him, and I took a garment secretly from my father's house, and gave it to him who was in distress.

16 Do you, therefore, my children, from that which God bestoweth upon you, show compassion and mercy without hesitation to all men, and give to every man with a good heart.

17 And if ye have not the wherewithal to give to him that needeth, have compassion for him in bowels of mercy.

18 I know that my hand found not the wherewithal to give to him that needed, and I walked with him weeping for seven furlongs, and my bowels yearned towards him in compassion.

19 Therefore my children, have compassion towards every man with mercy, that the Lord also may have compassion and mercy upon you.

20 Because also in the last days God will send His compassion on the earth, and wheresoever He findeth bowels of mercy He dwelleth in him.

21 For in the degree in which a man hath compassion upon his neighbours, in the same degree hath the Lord also upon him.

This is the same lesson King Benjamin gave. Give what you can, and if you can't give, foster within an attitude that you would give if you could.

22 And when we went down into Egypt, Joseph bore no malice against us.

23 To whom taking heed, do ye also, my children, approve yourselves without malice, and love one another; and do not set down in account, each one of you, evil against his brother.

24 For this breaketh unity and divideth all kindred, and troubleth the soul, and weareth away the countenance.

Joseph was not one *to keep score*, so to speak.

25 Observe the waters and know when they flow together, they sweep along stones, trees, earth, and other things.

26 But if they are divided into many streams, the earth swalloweth them up, and they vanish away.

27 So shall ye also be if ye be divided. Be not ye therefore divided into two heads for everything which the Lord made hath but one head, and two shoulders, two hands, two feet, and all the remaining members.

28 For I have learnt in the writing of my fathers, that ye shall be divided in Israel, and ye shall follow two kings, and shall work every abomination.

This indeed came to pass as Israel split into two kingdoms, Israel under the reign of Ephraim, and Judah under the command of Judah.

29 And your enemies shall lead you captive, and ye shall be evil entreated among the Gentiles with many infirmities and tribulations.

30 And after these things ye shall remember the Lord and repent, and He shall have mercy upon you, for He is merciful and compassionate.

31 And He setteth not down in account evil against the sons of men, because they are flesh, and are deceived through their own wicked deeds.

32 And after these things shall there arise unto you the Lord Himself, the light of righteousness, and ye shall return unto your land.

33 And ye shall see Him in Jerusalem, for His name's sake.

This is speaking of the Messiah Jesus Christ.

34 And again through the wickedness of your works shall ye provoke Him to anger,

35 And ye shall be cast away by Him unto the time of consummation.

This is astounding! One of the best prophecies of Jesus Christ outside of the work of the Restoration.

36 And now, my children, grieve not that I am dying, nor be cast down in that I am coming to my end.

37 For I shall rise again in the midst of you, as a ruler in the midst of his sons; and I shall rejoice in the midst of my tribe, as many as shall keep the law of the Lord, and the commandments of Zebulun their father.

38 But upon the ungodly shall the Lord bring eternal fire, and destroy them throughout all generations.

39 But I am now hastening away to my rest, as did also my fathers.

40 But do ye fear the Lord our God with all your strength all the days of your life.

41 And when he had said these things he fell asleep, at a good old age.

42 And his sons laid him in a wooden coffin. And afterwards they carried him up and buried him in Hebron with his fathers.

Genesis 46:14 And the sons of Zebulun; Sered, and Elon, and Jahleel.

15 These be the sons of Leah, which she bare unto Jacob in Padan-aram, with his daughter Dinah: all the souls of his sons and his daughters were thirty and three.

LATTER-DAY LESSONS FROM FATHER ZEBULUN

It is interesting to note that both Issachar and Zebulun, the two sons which Leah bought for mandrakes, were the brothers with the deepest compassion for Joseph in his time of need. We learn from these writings that Judah was a better man than the Bible portrays him, Levi and Reuben too. The real piece of work in Leah's family was Simeon, who would have been unquestionably number 2 in terms of family hierarchy until Joseph was born. The number one sons of both Bilhah and Zilpah also hated Joseph. We learn from these testimonies that the rest of the brothers were better men than the Bible portrays them. Zebulun teaches the pain of regret. It is one thing to feel the guilt of sin committed, it is another thing to look back with regret about what might have been. In trying to keep the peace or not make waves, Zebulun found himself pained that he was not brave enough to stand up to injustice. And what injustice it was! To plot to murder or sale your own flesh and blood. It is a terrible thing.

Zebulun did have the most compassion and in that was the most Christlike of the brothers involved in Joseph's sale. Note how he is also a man of vision and heavenly dreams. The Lord is this way and like adheres to like. If one wishes to have greater spirituality, one needs to strive to be like the Lord and the Lord will come with His spiritual gifts.

It is interesting to note that Zebulun teaches that there will be a resurrection. This should be of comfort to our brothers of the Jewish faith but when one considers that Ezekiel teaches the same thing and they still don't believe it answers the question of the Lord Himself:

Luke 16:31 If they hear not Moses and the prophets, neither will they be persuaded, though one rose from the dead.

Amen, Lord, amen.

From Father Jacob:

Genesis 49:13 Zebulun shall dwell at the haven of the sea; and he shall be for an haven of ships; and his border shall be unto Zidon.

Moses told his tribe to "Rejoice, Zebulun, in thy going out." We assume he meant "going out to sea."

Detail of The Remorse of Orestes by William Adolphe
Bouguereau, 1862.

Chapter Seven

Dan

Understand ye my sons that the power of wrath is vain. For anger is blindness, and does not suffer one to see the face of any man with truth. Keep, therefore, yourselves, my children, from every evil work, and cast away wrath and all lying, and love truth and long-suffering. — Dan

Dan was the seventh son born to Jacob. His mother was Bilhah, Rachel's maid. When Rachel was unable to have children, she decided to follow Sarah's pattern and try to have a family through a surrogate. Dan struggled with terrible anger issues. He seems to have put this anger onto young Joseph. We do know from other sources that Leah's sons treated Dan like a servant but that being a younger brother he looked up to Leah's sons. When Joseph was born, his status as Jacob's other eldest son via Rachel by surrogacy was seriously compromised. Now he was the eldest son of a servant, making a mere boy – Joseph – his legal master. Dan's essay on masculine anger and its effects are masterfully laid out here. He comes to understand that wrath is only useful in the end to Satan.

Dan 1:1 The copy of the words of Dan, which he spake to his sons in his last days, in the hundred and twenty-fifth year of his life.

2 For he called together his family, and said: Hearken to my words, ye sons of Dan; and give heed to the words of your father.

3 I have proved in my heart, and in my whole life, that truth and dealing justly is good and well pleasing to God, and that lying and anger are evil, because they teach man all wickedness.

4 I confess, therefore, this day to you, my children, that in my heart I resolved on the death of Joseph my brother, the true and good man.

5 And I rejoiced that he was sold, because our father loved him more than us.

6 For the spirit of jealousy and vainglory said to me: Thou thyself also art his son.

7 And one of the spirits of Beliar stirred me up, saying: Take this sword, and with it slay Joseph: so shall thy father love thee when he is dead.

8 Now this is the spirit of anger that persuaded me to crush Joseph as a leopard crusheth a kid.

9 But the God of my fathers did not suffer him to fall into my hands, so that I should find him alone and slay him, and cause a second tribe to be destroyed in Israel.

10 And now, my children, behold I am dying, and I tell you of a truth, that unless ye keep yourselves from the spirit of lying and of anger, and love truth and longsuffering, ye shall perish.

11 For anger is blindness, and does not suffer one to see the face of any man with truth.

12 For though it be a father or a mother, he behaveth towards them as enemies; though it be a brother, he knoweth him not; though it be a prophet of the Lord, he disobeyeth him; though a righteous man, he regardeth him not; though a friend, he doth not acknowledge him.

13 For the spirit of anger encompasseth him with the net of deceit, and blindeth his eyes, and through lying darkeneth his mind, and giveth him its own peculiar vision.

14 And wherewith encompasseth it his eyes? With hatred of heart, so as to be envious of his brother.

15 For anger is an evil thing, my children, for it troubleth even the soul itself.

16 And the body of the angry man it maketh its own, and over his soul it getteth the mastery, and it bestoweth upon the body power that it may work all iniquity.

17 And when the body does all these things, the soul justifieth what is done, since it seeth not aright.

18 Therefore he that is wrathful, if he be a mighty man, hath a threefold power in his anger: one by the help of his servants; and a second by his wealth, whereby he persuadeth and overcometh wrongfully; and thirdly, having his own natural power he worketh thereby the evil.

19 And though the wrathful man be weak, yet hath he a power twofold of that which is by nature; for wrath ever aideth such in lawlessness.

20 This spirit goeth always with lying at the right hand of Satan, that with cruelty and lying his works may be wrought.

21 Understand ye, therefore, the power of wrath, that it is vain.

22 For it first of all giveth provocation by word; then by deeds it strengtheneth him who is angry, and with sharp losses disturbeth his mind, and so stirreth up with great wrath his soul.

23 Therefore, when any one speaketh against you, be not ye moved to anger, and if any man praiseth you as holy men, be not uplifted: be not moved either to delight or to disgust.

24 For first it pleaseth the hearing, and so maketh the mind keen to perceive the grounds for provocation; and then being enraged, he thinketh that he is justly angry.

25 If ye fall into any loss or ruin, my children, be not afflicted; for this very spirit maketh a man desire that which is perishable, in order that he may be enraged through the affliction.

26 And if ye suffer loss voluntarily, or involuntarily, be not vexed; for from vexation ariseth wrath with lying.

27 Moreover, a twofold mischief is wrath with lying; and they assist one another in order to disturb the heart; and when the soul is continually disturbed, the Lord departeth from it, and Beliar ruleth over it.

Dan will leave his children an important prophecy outlining the sins, captivity, and plagues that will come upon the people. Somethings never change. The children of men still long for Eden and to go home to God in peace.

Dan 2:1 Observe, therefore, my children, the commandments of the Lord, and keep His law; depart from wrath, and hate lying, that the Lord may dwell among you, and Beliar may flee from you.

2 Speak truth each one with his neighbour. So shall ye not fall into wrath and confusion; but ye shall be in peace, having the God of peace, so shall no war prevail over you.

3 Love the Lord through all your life, and one another with a true heart.

4 I know that in the last days ye shall depart from the Lord, and ye shall provoke Levi unto anger, and fight against Judah; but ye shall not prevail

against them, for an angel of the Lord shall guide them both; for by them shall Israel stand.[26]

Dan was the first to cause trouble in Israel when he introduced foreign wives and their idols into the Holy Land.

5 And whensoever ye depart from the Lord, ye shall walk in all evil and work the abominations of the Gentiles, going a-whoring after women of the lawless ones, while with all wickedness the spirits of wickedness work in you.

The tribe of Dan would be the first to weaken Israel after the Exodus when they sought foreign women and followed them in false worship. According to the *Order of Heaven*, a man is supposed to lead out in religious matters in the home. Dan would change this and in order to please foreign wives, bring destruction upon the entire family.

6 For I have read in the book of Enoch the righteous, that your prince will be Satan, and that all the spirits of wickedness and pride will conspire to attend constantly on the sons of Levi, to cause them to sin before the Lord.[27]

7 And my sons will draw near to Levi, and sin with them in all things; and the sons of Judah will be covetous, plundering other men's goods like lions.

8 Therefore shall ye be led away with them into captivity, and there shall ye receive all the plagues of Egypt, and all the evils of the Gentiles.

9 And so when ye return to the Lord ye shall obtain mercy, and He shall bring you into His sanctuary, and He shall give you peace.

10 And there shall arise unto you from the tribe of Judah and of Levi the salvation of the Lord; and he shall make war against Beliar.[28]

This is speaking of Jesus Christ and John the Baptist. It is interesting to note how this says that until the earthly ministries of these men, Satan had none to really molest his interests nor to make his kingdom afraid.

11 And execute an everlasting vengeance on our enemies; and the captivity shall he take from Beliar the souls of the saints, and turn disobedient hearts unto the Lord, and give to them that call upon him eternal peace.

12 And the saints shall rest in Eden, and in the New Jerusalem shall the righteous rejoice, and it shall be unto the glory of God for ever.

13 And no longer shall Jerusalem endure desolation, nor Israel be led captive; for the Lord shall be in the midst of it [living amongst men], and the Holy One of Israel shall reign over it in humility and in poverty; and he who believeth on Him shall reign amongst men in truth.

14 And now, fear the Lord, my children, and beware of Satan and his spirits.

15 Draw near unto God and unto the angel that intercedeth for you, for he is a mediator between God and man, and for the peace of Israel he shall stand up against the kingdom of the enemy.

16 Therefore is the enemy eager to destroy all that call upon the Lord.

17 For he knoweth that upon the day on which Israel shall repent, the kingdom of the enemy shall be brought to an end.[29]

Wow! We know that Satan desires to destroy all who pray. Why? Because He knows that the Lord is quick to hear and forgive. Once men truly forgive one another, the Lord will be quick to forgive us all. Once we can hear the word of the Lord and do it, Lucifer's kingdom will be over. Specifically we are told that he knows that the children of Israel will be forgiven. When they ask for it as a nation, Lucifer's kingdom is over.

18 For the very angel of peace shall strengthen Israel, that it fall not into the extremity of evil.

19 And it shall be in the time of the lawlessness of Israel, that the Lord will not depart from them, but will transform them into a nation that doeth His will, for none of the angels will be equal unto him.

20 And His name shall be in every place in Israel, and among the Gentiles.[30]

21 Keep, therefore, yourselves, my children, from every evil work, and cast away wrath and all lying, and love truth and long-suffering.

22 And the things which ye have heard from your father, do ye also impart to your children that the Saviour of the Gentiles may receive you; for he is true and long-suffering, meek and lowly, and teacheth by his works the law of God.

Dan is saying that the Lord will also save the nations. Gentile simply means nations. Here he is testifying of the Lord's commission first to Peter, and then to Joseph Smith, to save the nations in His holy name. Dan is telling his children to watch for the sign of the one who will reach out to the nations, He will be the Messiah and the Messiah's true servants.

23 Depart, therefore, from all unrighteousness, and cleave unto the righteousness of God, and our tribe will be saved for ever.

24 And bury me near my fathers.

25 And when he had said these things he kissed them, and fell asleep at a good old age.

26 And his sons buried him, and after that they carried up his bones, and placed them near Abraham, and Isaac, and Jacob.

27 Nevertheless, Dan prophesied unto them that they should forget their God, and should be alienated from the land of their inheritance and from the race of Israel, and from the family of their seed.

Genesis 46:23 And the sons of Dan; Hushim.

Jubilee says that Dan had six sons but that five died in the year they travelled to Egypt, leaving only Hushim.

Jubilees 44:28 And the sons of Dan were Hushim, and Sâmôn, and Asûdî, and 'Îjâka, and Salômôn – six.

29 And they died the year in which they entered into Egypt, and there was left to Dan Hushim alone.

LATTER-DAY LESSONS FROM FATHER DAN

As a tribe, the Lord has had a lot of trouble with Dan. They seem to the be ones who struggle the most with idolatry, a sin which is especially egregious for Israel in that they have committed themselves to loving none but the Lord God. In this respect, idolatry is symbolically adultery when practiced by Israel.

Mormons will note that Dan speaks about the New Jerusalem. This is particularly wonderful here because in later prophecy about the New Jerusalem, Dan is sometimes left out as a means of saying that there will be no idolatry in the New Jerusalem. Note this wonderful tidbit from the Prophet Joseph Smith:

The City of Zion, spoken of by David in the 102nd psalm, will be built upon the land of America, and the ransomed of the Lord shall return and come to it with songs of everlasting joy upon their heads. And then they will be delivered from the over-flowing scourge that shall pass through the land. But Judah shall obtain deliverance at Jerusalem.[31]

Father Jacob left his son this:

Genesis 49:16 Dan shall judge his people, as one of the tribes of Israel.

17 Dan shall be a serpent by the way, an adder in the path, that biteth the horse heels, so that his rider shall fall backward.

18 I have waited for thy salvation, O Lord.

This is the most cryptic of the blessing/prophecies left by Israel. Traditionally it has been seen as speaking of the Anti-Christ. Roman Catholics, noting that one of the Greek tribes called themselves the Danii, and claimed kinship to Israel through Dan, used that to say that the Anti-Christ would rise from the Greek Orthodox Church. The Orthodox movement countered by calling the Pope the Anti-Christ. Logic dictates that in the future Dan may hold the civil authority of the courts over the tribes of Israel, just as Levi oversees the priestly duties.

Let's add in Moses:

Deuteronomy 33:22 Dan is a lion's whelp: he shall leap from Bashan.

I think this is saying that despite Dan's anger and the idol worship which his children would later bring into Israel, they would in the end come around, repent, and be listed forever in the Holy City with the other tribes. Rabbis have traditionally read these verses as pertaining to the Reign of the Judges in the days before King Saul and as being Samson in particular.

Chapter Eight

Naphtali

For as the potter knoweth the vessel, how much it is to contain, and bringeth clay accordingly, so also doth the Lord make the body after the likeness of the spirit, and according to the capacity of the body doth He implant the spirit. For there is no inclination or thought which the Lord knoweth not, for He created every man after His own image. — Naphtali

Naphtali was the sixth son born to Father Israel and the second son with Rachel's maid Bilhah. He was named by Rachel Naphtali, meaning "my struggle." Wanting a child of her own was Rachel's greatest struggle as matriarch. It is said that he was a very swift runner and that may be why his father assigned him the totem symbol of the hind, old English for a Red Deer, an herbivore more in the family of an elk.

Naphtali 1:1 The copy of the testament of Naphtali, which he ordained at the time of his death in the hundred and thirtieth year of his life.

2 When his sons were gathered together in the seventh month, on the first day of the month, while still in good health, he made them a feast of food and wine.

3 And after he was awake in the morning, he said to them, "I am dying;" and they believed him not.

4 And as he glorified the Lord, he grew strong and said that after yesterday's feast he should die.

5 And he began then to say: Hear, my children, ye sons of Naphtali, hear the words of your father.

6 I was born from Bilhah, and because Rachel dealt craftily, and gave Bilhah in place of herself to Jacob, and she conceived and bare me upon Rachel's knees, therefore she called my name Naphtali.

7 For Rachel loved me very much because I was born upon her lap; and when I was still young she was wont to kiss me, and say: "May I have a brother of thine from mine own womb, like unto thee."

8 Whence also Joseph was like unto me in all things, according to the prayers of Rachel.

9 Now my mother was Bilhah, daughter of Rotheus the brother of Deborah, Rebecca's nurse, who was born on one and the self-same day with Rachel.

10 And Rotheus was of the family of Abraham, a Chaldean, God-fearing, free-born, and noble.

11 And he was taken captive and was bought by Laban; and he gave him Euna his handmaid to wife, and she bore a daughter, and called her name Zilpah, after the name of the village in which he had been taken captive.

12 And next she bore Bilhah, saying: My daughter hastens after what is new, for immediately that she was born she seized the breast and hastened to suck it.

13 And I was swift on my feet like the deer, and my father Jacob appointed me for all messages, and as a deer did he give me his blessing.

14 For as the potter knoweth the vessel, how much it is to contain, and bringeth clay accordingly, so also doth the Lord make the body after the likeness of the spirit, and according to the capacity of the body doth He implant the spirit.

15 And the one does not fall short of the other by a third part of a hair; for by weight, and measure, and rule was all the creation made.

16 And as the potter knoweth the use of each vessel, what it is meet for, so also doth the Lord know the body, how far it will persist in goodness, and when it beginneth in evil.

17 For there is no inclination or thought which the Lord knoweth not, for He created every man after His own image.

18 For as a man's strength, so also in his work; as his eye, so also in his sleep; as his soul, so also in his word either in the law of the Lord or in the law of Beliar.

19 And as there is a division between light and darkness, between seeing and hearing, so also is there a division between man and man, and between woman and woman; and it is not to be said that the one is like the other either in face or in mind.[32]

20 For God made all things good in their order, the five senses in the head, and He joined on the neck to the head, adding to it the hair also for comeliness and glory, then the heart for understanding, the belly for excrement, and the stomach for grinding, the windpipe for taking in the breath,

the liver for wrath, the gall for bitterness, the spleen for laughter, the reins for prudence, the muscles of the loins for power, the lungs for drawing in, the loins for strength, and so forth.

21 So then, my children, let all your works be done in order with good intent in the fear of God, and do nothing disorderly in scorn or out of its due season.

22 For if thou bid the eye to hear, it cannot; so neither while ye are in darkness can ye do the works of light.[33]

23 Be ye, therefore, not eager to corrupt your doings through covetousness or with vain words to beguile your souls; because if ye keep silence in purity of heart, ye shall understand how to hold fast the will of God, and to cast away the will of Beliar.

24 The sun and moon and stars change not the commands of the Lord in their flight among the heavens; so ye change not the law of God though your paths be disorder. They fulfill their purpose. Ye fulfill yours.[34]

25 The Gentiles went astray, and forsook the Lord, and charged their order, and obeyed sticks and stones, and the spirits of deceit.

26 But ye shall not be so, my children, recognizing in the firmament, in the earth, and in the sea, and in all created things, the Lord who made all things, that ye become not as Sodom, which changed the order of nature, lusting man to man.

27 In like manner the Watchers also changed the order of their nature, whom the Lord cursed at the flood, on whose account He made the earth without inhabitants and fruitless.

28 These things I say unto you, my children, for I have read in the writing of Enoch that ye yourselves also shall depart from the Lord, walking according to all the lawlessness of the Gentiles, and ye shall do according to all the wickedness of Sodom.

29 And the Lord shall bring captivity upon you, and there shall ye serve your enemies, and ye shall be bowed down with every affliction and tribulation, until the Lord have consumed you all.

30 And after ye have become diminished and made few, ye will return and acknowledge the Lord your God; and He shall bring you back into your land, according to His abundant mercy.

31 And it shall be, that after that they come into the land of their fathers, they shall again forget the Lord and become ungodly.

32 And the Lord shall scatter them upon the face of all the earth, until the compassion of the Lord shall come, a man working righteousness and working mercy unto all them that are afar off, and to them that are near.

THE VISION OF NAPHTALI

Naphtali 2:1 For in the fortieth year of my life, I saw a vision on the Mount of Olives, on the east of Jerusalem, that the sun and the moon were standing still.

2 And behold Isaac, the father of my father, said to us; Run and lay hold of them, each one according to his strength; and to him that seizeth them will the sun and moon belong.

3 And we all of us ran together, and Levi laid hold of the sun, and Judah outstripped the others and seized the moon, and they were both of them lifted up with them.[35]

4 And when Levi became as a sun, lo, a certain young man gave to him twelve branches of palm; and Judah was bright as the moon, and under their feet were twelve rays.

5 And the two, Levi and Judah, ran, and laid hold of them.

6 And lo, a bull upon the earth, with two great horns, and an eagle's wings upon its back; and we wished to seize him, but could not.

7 But Joseph came, and seized him, and ascended up with him on high.

In other words, what the kings and priests of Israel could not accomplish, Joseph would do with both the Melchizedek Priesthood (via Joseph Smith) and the Eagle (the church in waiting in the wilderness). Joseph, through Ephraim, would master the nations but his greatest foil would be Esau. We are witnessing the fulfillment of this prophecy even now.[36]

8 And I saw, for I was there, and behold a holy writing appeared to us, saying: Assyrians, Medes, Persians, Chaldeans, Syrians, shall possess in captivity the twelve tribes of Israel.

But before that day, the nations would cause Israel to sorrow for their disobedience.

9 And again, after seven days, I saw our father Jacob standing by the sea of Jamnia, and we were with him.

10 And behold, there came a ship sailing by, without sailors or pilot; and there was written upon the ship, *The Ship of Jacob.*

11 And our father said to us: Come, let us embark on our ship.

12 And when he had gone on board, there arose a vehement storm, and a mighty tempest of wind; and our father, who was holding the helm, departed from us.

13 And we, being tossed with the tempest, were borne along over the sea; and the ship was filled with water, and was pounded by mighty waves, until it was broken up.

14 And Joseph fled away upon a little boat, and we were all divided upon nine planks, and Levi and Judah were together.

15 And we were all scattered unto the ends of the earth.

This occurred with the loss of the Ten Tribes in the days of the Assyrian captivity and again when Father Lehi left the Holy Land for the Americas.

16 Then Levi, girt about with sackcloth, prayed for us all unto the Lord.

17 And when the storm ceased, the ship reached the land as it were in peace.

18 And, lo, our father came, and we all rejoiced with one accord.

19 These two dreams I told to my father; and he said to me: These things must be fulfilled in their season, after that Israel hath endured many things.

Then this interesting insight by Jacob, which must have puzzled him some:

20 Then my father saith unto me: "I believe God that Joseph liveth, for I see always that the Lord numbereth him with you."

21 And he said, weeping: "Ah me, my son Joseph, thou livest, though I behold thee not, and thou seest not Jacob that begat thee."

You will remember that Joseph's body was never found. His brothers showed up with his bloody coat and said, "Father we found this coat along the barren road, the very road that you send your 17 year old son along without escort nor protection.

93

We think it is Joseph's coat. What do you think? Notice the blood and tear marks like some horrible beast ate him." No body was found. So, could Joseph be alive out there somewhere? Parents who have lost children without a corpse all say that not knowing is the worst part of it all.

22 He caused me also, therefore, to weep by these words, and I burned in my heart to declare that Joseph had been sold, but I feared my brethren.

23 Now my children, I have shown unto you the last times, how everything shall come to pass in Israel.

24 Do ye also, therefore, charge your children that they be united to Levi and to Judah; for through them shall salvation arise unto Israel, and in them shall Jacob be blessed.

25 For through their tribes shall God appear dwelling among men on earth, to save the race of Israel, and to gather together the righteous from amongst the Gentiles.

26 If ye work that which is good, my children, both men and angels shall bless you; and God shall be glorified among the Gentiles through you, and the devil shall flee from you, and the wild beasts shall fear you, and the Lord shall love you, and the angels shall cleave to you.

Had Israel stayed united, they would have become the most powerful nation for good in all the world; but the Lord had a plan to save them a second time. It was a plan that He showed them in secret symbol. Just as Joseph had been sold into the wilderness while Judah, Levi, and all the rest suffered in their ignorance and separation, only to find tearful Joseph waiting in preparation to save them, so it should be again in our day. Joseph waits for Israel in the wilderness against the New World's Dead Salty Sea.

27 As a man who has trained a child well is kept in kindly remembrance; so also for a good work there is a good remembrance before God.

28 But him that doeth not that which is good, both angels and men shall curse, and God shall be dishonoured among the Gentiles through him, and the devil

shall make him as his own peculiar instrument, and every wild beast shall master him, and the Lord shall hate him.

This was the Lord's exact point to Ezekiel. Israel had caused His name to "stink" before the nations. This He could not allow and so He punished them under the hands of Nebuchadnezzar and the other Gentile kings.

29 For the commandments of the law are twofold, and through prudence must they be fulfilled.

30 For there is a season for a man to embrace his wife, and a season to abstain therefrom for his prayer.

31 So, then, there are two commandments; and, unless they be done in due order, they bring very great sin upon men.

32 So also is it with the other commandments.

33 Be ye therefore wise in God, my children, and prudent, understanding the order of His commandments, and the laws of every word, that the Lord may love you,

34 And when he had charged them with many such words, he exhorted them that they should remove his bones to Hebron, and that they should bury him with his fathers.

35 And when he had eaten and drunken with a merry heart, he covered his face and died.

36 And his sons did according to all that Naphtali their Father had commanded them.

Genesis 46:24 And the sons of Naphtali; Jahzeel, and Guni, and Jezer, and Shillem.

25 These are the sons of Bilhah, which Laban gave unto Rachel his daughter, and she bare these unto Jacob: all the souls were seven.

LATTER-DAY LESSONS FROM FATHER NAPHTALI

Naphtali warned his sons that they would be tempted by the sins of Sodom. While sodomy was a real practice by the men of the city, you will note that Naphtali speaks of Sodom's sins; in the plural. The Five Cities of the Plain, which included Sodom, were known for their drug trade, their petroleum resources, their heavy taxation and their cruelty to strangers, all in addition to their sexual practices. The Lord's hatred for Sodom is here clearly explained by Naphtali as being connected to His hatred for the Watchers. You may remember from our *Gospel Feast Vol. 7: Genesis & the Sons of the Morning* that ultimately Noah's flood was brought about by the near complete domination of the planet by the cult of the Watchers. We know them as the cult of Mahan, started by Lucifer and Cain. This cult successfully created a world paradigm which so effectively competed with our Heavenly Father's Plan of Salvation, that in time only Noah, his wife, their 3 sons and their wives were unaffected by it.

This very same cult of Mahan, which taught that heavenly angels with great knowledge left their abode in heaven, and enacted sodomitic practices on men and women on earth leading to a race of super beings, still functions among us today as tales of aliens come down from the skies with their anal probes and their star children born of human women. It is the same cult from the same demonic mastermind re-imagineered for the modern age. While modern men scoff at our forebears for their myths of the Anunnaki, Zeus and Ganymede, we watch in awe the same skies for Venusian Tall Whites, Reptilians, Aryans, Little Greys, and Mothmen. It is the same mythology. Naphtali's testimony also attaches the Mahanistic practice of "seeding a child with a demon" to the Watchers, which is something we discussed in our studies of the pre-flood world.[37]

Naphtali also validates the initial vision given many years later to Gad the Seer of David. Please see *Gad the Seer & the Corruption of the Covenant* for more information.

Naphtali tells his children that the Messiah will be the ultimate Teacher of Righteousness, a title we explored together in our feast on *Zechariah*.

Jacob left this blessing:

Genesis 49:21 Naphtali is a hind let loose: he giveth goodly words.

Moses said, "O Naphtali, satisfied with favour, and full with the blessing of the Lord: possess thou the west and the south."

The red deer (Cervus elaphus) is one of the largest deer species.

Chapter Nine

Gad

Righteousness casteth out hatred. Humility destroyeth envy. — *Gad*

Gad was the ninth son of Jacob through Zilpah. He was a shepherd and a very strong man but he struggled with hatred and had a murderous heart. He did overcome himself in time. Leah's sons were not nice to Zilpah's children. Where at least until the birth of Joseph, Bilhah's sons were considered Rachel's, Gad and his brother Asher, being Zilpah's, were treated like dogs in the eyes of Leah's sons.

Gad 1:1 The copy of the testament of Gad, what things he spake unto his sons, in the hundred and twenty-fifth year of his life, saying unto them:

2 Hearken, my children, I was the seventh son born to Jacob, and I was valiant in keeping the flocks.

3 Accordingly I guarded at night the flock; and whenever the lion came, or the wolf, or any wild beast against the fold, I pursued it, and overtaking it I seized its foot with my hand and hurled it about a stone's throw, and so killed it.

4 Now Joseph my brother was feeding the flock with us for upwards of thirty days, and being young, he fell sick by reason of the heat.

5 And he returned to Hebron to our father, who made him lie down near him, because he loved him greatly.

6 And Joseph told our father that the sons of Zilpah and Bilhah were slaying the best of the flock and eating them against the judgement of Reuben and Judah.

7 For he saw that I had delivered a lamb out of the mouth of a bear, and put the bear to death; but had slain the lamb, being grieved concerning it that it could not live, and that we had eaten it.

8 And regarding this matter I was wroth with Joseph until the day that he was sold.

9 And the spirit of hatred was in me, and I wished not either to hear of Joseph with the ears, or see him with the eyes, because he rebuked us to our faces saying that we were eating of the flock without Judah.

10 For whatsoever things he told our father, he believed him.

11 I confess now my sin, my children, that oftentimes I wished to kill him, because I hated him from my heart.

12 Moreover, I hated him yet more for his dreams; and I wished to lick him out of the land of the living, even as an ox licketh up the grass of the field.

13 But Judah sold him to the Ishmaelites.

14 Thus the God of our fathers delivered him from our hands, that we should not work great lawlessness in Israel.

15 And now, my children, hearken to the words of truth to work righteousness, and all the law of the Most High, and go not astray through the spirit of hatred, for it is evil in all the doings of men.

16 Whatsoever a man doeth the hater abominateth him: and though a man worketh the law of the Lord, he praiseth him not; though a man feareth the Lord, and taketh pleasure in that which is righteous, he loveth him not.

17 He dispraiseth the truth, he envieth him that prospereth, he welcometh evil-speaking, he loveth arrogance, for hatred blindeth his soul; as I also then looked on Joseph.

18 Beware, therefore, my children of hatred, for it worketh lawlessness even against the Lord Himself.

19 For it will not hear the words of His commandments concerning the loving of one's neighbour, and it sinneth against God.

20 For if a brother stumble, it delighteth immediately to proclaim it to all men, and is urgent that he should be judged for it, and be punished and be put to death.

21 And if it be a servant it stirreth him up against his master, and with every affliction it deviseth against him, if possibly he can be put to death.

22 For hatred worketh with envy also against them that prosper: so long as it heareth of or seeth their success it always languisheth.

23 For as love would quicken even the dead, and would call back them that are condemned to die, so hatred would slay the living, and those who had sinned to a small degree, it would condemn to death.

24 For the spirit of hatred worketh together with Satan, through hastiness of spirits, in all things to men's death; but the spirit of love worketh together with the law of God in long-suffering unto the salvation of men.

Note this fascinating summation of hatred by one who struggled with it and at last overcame it.

25 Hatred, therefore, is evil, for it constantly mateth with lying, speaking against the truth; and it maketh small things to be great, and causeth the light to be darkness, and calleth the sweet bitter, and teacheth slander, and kindleth wrath, and stirreth up war, and violence and all covetousness; it filleth the heart with evils and devilish poison.

This is no small achievement. Lucifer was filled with hate and he has never overcome it.

26 These things, therefore, I say to you from experience, my children, that ye may drive forth hatred, which is of the devil, and cleave to the love of God.

27 Righteousness casteth out hatred, humility destroyeth envy.

28 For he that is just and humble is ashamed to do what is unjust, being reproved not of another, but of his own heart, because the Lord looketh on his inclination.

29 He speaketh not against a holy man, because the fear of God overcometh hatred.

30 For fearing lest he should offend the Lord, he will not do wrong to any man, even in thought.

31 These things I learnt at last, after I had repented concerning Joseph.

32 For true repentance after a godly sort destroyeth ignorance, and driveth away the darkness, and enlighteneth the eyes, and giveth knowledge to the soul, and leadeth the mind to salvation.

33 And those things which it hath not learnt from man, it knoweth through repentance.

34 For God brought upon me a disease of the liver; and had not the prayers of Jacob my father succoured me, it had hardly failed but my spirit had departed.

35 For by what things a man transgresseth by the same also is he punished .

36 Since, therefore, my liver was set mercilessly against Joseph, in my liver too I suffered mercilessly, and was judged for eleven months, for so long a time as I had been angry against Joseph.

God 2:1 And now, my children, I exhort you, love ye each one his brother, and put away hatred from your hearts, love one another in deed, and in word, and in the inclination of the soul.

2 For in the presence of my father I spake peaceably to Joseph; and when I had gone out, the spirit of hatred darkened my mind, and stirred up my soul to slay him.

3 Love ye one another from the heart; and if a man sin against thee, speak peaceably to him, and in thy soul hold not guile; and if he repent and confess, forgive him.

4 But if he deny it, do not get into a passion with him, lest catching the poison from thee he take to swearing and so thou sin doubly.

5 Let not another man hear thy secrets when engaged in legal strife, lest he come to hate thee and become thy enemy, and commit a great sin against thee; for ofttimes such as he will addresseth thee guilefully or busieth himself about thee but hath wicked intent.

6 And though he deny it and yet have a sense of shame when reproved, see to it that thou reprove him.

7 For he who denieth may repent so as not again to wrong thee; yea, he may also honour thee, and fear and be at peace with thee.

8 And if he be shameless and persist in his wrong-doing, even so forgive him from the heart, and leave to God the avenging.

9 If a man prospereth more than you, do not be vexed, but pray also for him, that he may have greater prosperity, for so it is expedient for you.

10 And if he be further exalted, be not envious of him, remembering that all flesh shall die; and offer praise to God, who giveth things good and profitable to all men.

11 Seek out the judgments of the Lord, and thy mind will rest and be at peace.

12 And though a man become rich by evil means, even as Esau, the brother of my father, be not jealous; but wait for the end of the Lord.

13 For the Lord will take away from such a man his wealth gotten by evil means or punish him if he will not repent; or He forgiveth him if he doth repent, but the unrepentant is reserved for eternal punishment.

14 For the poor man free from envy pleaseth the Lord in all things. He is blessed beyond all men, because he hath not the travail of vain men.

15 Put away, therefore, jealousy from your souls, and love one another with uprightness of heart.

16 Do ye also therefore tell these things to your children, that they honour Judah and Levi, for from them shall the Lord raise up salvation to Israel.

17 For I know that at the last your children shall depart from Him, and shall walk in wickedness, and affliction and corruption before the Lord.

18 And when he had rested for a little while, he said again; My children, obey your father, and bury me near to my fathers.

19 And he drew up his feet, and fell asleep in peace.

20 And after five years they carried him up to Hebron, and laid him with his fathers.

Genesis 46:16 And the sons of Gad; Ziphion, and Haggi, Shuni, and Ezbon, Eri, and Arodi, and Areli.

LATTER-DAY LESSONS FROM FATHER GAD

Gad reaffirms the testimony of his brothers that it was clearly taught to watch within Judah's house for the birth of the Messiah. Father Jacob left this for Gad:

Genesis 49:19 Gad, a troop shall overcome him: but he shall overcome at the last.

It's wonderful to see how holy writ holds together. Go back and re-read *Issachar 1:43-44*. Moses added this blessing:

Deuteronomy 33:20... Blessed be he that enlargeth Gad: he dwelleth as a lion, and teareth the arm with the crown of the head.

21 And he provided the first part for himself, because there, in a portion of the lawgiver, was he seated; and he came with the heads of the people, he executed the justice of the Lord, and his judgments with Israel.

Chapter Ten

Asher

My children wear not two faces. Destroy the evil inclination by your good works; for they that are double-faced serve not God. Keep the law of the Lord, and give not heed unto evil as unto good; but look unto the thing that is really good, and keep it in all commandments of the Lord. — *Asher*

Asher was the tenth son of Jacob and Zilpah. His final words are brief but powerful. He speaks about the dangers of duality which we might call hypocrisy. Asher proves himself to be a deep thinker.

Asher 1:1 The copy of the Testament of Asher, what things he spake to his sons in the hundred and twenty-fifth year of his life.

2 For while he was still in health, he said to them: Hearken, ye children of Asher, to your father, and I will declare to you all that is upright in the sight of the Lord.

3 Two ways hath God given to the sons of men, and two inclinations, and two kinds of action, and two modes of action, and two issues.

4 Therefore all things are by twos, one over against the other.

5 For there are two ways: good and evil, and with these are the two inclinations in our breasts discriminating them.

6 Therefore if the soul take pleasure in the good inclination, all its actions are in righteousness; and if it sin it straightway repenteth.

This is one of the first concepts the Lord would preach.

7 For, having its thoughts set upon righteousness, and casting away wickedness, it straightway overthroweth the evil, and uprooteth the sin.

8 But if it incline to the evil inclination, all its actions are in wickedness, and it driveth away the good, and cleaveth to the evil, and is ruled by Beliar; even though it work what is good, he perverteth it to evil.

9 For whenever it beginneth to do good, he forceth the issue of the action into evil for him, seeing that the treasure of the inclination is filled with an evil spirit.

10 A person then may with words help the good for the sake of the evil, yet the issue of the action leadeth to mischief.

11 There is a man who showeth no compassion upon him who serveth his turn in evil; and this thing hath two aspects, but the whole is evil.

12 And there is a man that loveth him that worketh evil, because he would prefer even to die in evil for his sake; and concerning this it is clear that it hath two aspects, but the whole is an evil work.

13 Though indeed he have love, yet is he wicked who concealeth what is evil for the sake of the good name, but the end of the action tendeth unto evil.

14 Another stealeth, doeth unjustly, plundereth, defraudeth, and withal pitieth the poor: this too hath a twofold aspect, but the whole is evil.

15 He who defraudeth his neighbour provoketh God, and sweareth falsely against the Most High, and yet pitieth the poor: the Lord who commanded the law he setteth at nought and provoketh, and yet he refresheth the poor.

16 He defileth the soul, and maketh gay the body; he killeth many, and pitieth a few: this, too, hath a twofold aspect, but the whole is evil.

17 Another committeth adultery and fornication, and abstaineth from meats, and when he fasteth he doeth evil, and by the power of his wealth overwhelmeth many; and notwithstanding his excessive wickedness he doeth the commandments: this, too, hath a twofold aspect, but the whole is evil.

18 Such men are hares; clean like those that divide the hoof, but in very deed are unclean.

19 For God in the tables of the commandments hath thus declared.

20 But do not ye, my children, wear two faces like unto them, of goodness and of wickedness; but cleave unto goodness only, for God hath his habitation therein, and men desire it.

21 But from wickedness flee away, destroying the evil inclination by your good works; for they that are double-faced serve not God, but their own lusts, so that they may please Beliar and men like unto themselves.

22 For good men, even they that are of single face, though they be thought by them that are double-faced to sin, are just before God.

23 For many in killing the wicked do two works, of good and evil; but the whole is good, because he hath uprooted and destroyed that which is evil.

24 One man hateth the merciful and unjust man, and the man who committeth adultery and fasteth: this, too, hath a twofold aspect, but the whole work is good, because he followeth the Lord's example, in that he accepteth not the seeming good as the genuine good.

25 Another desireth not to see good day with them that not, lest he defile his body and pollute his soul; this, too, is double-faced, but the whole is good.

26 For such men are like stags and does, because in the manner of wild animals they seem to be unclean, but they are altogether clean; because they walk in zeal for the Lord and abstain from what God also hateth and forbiddeth by His commandments, warding off the evil from the good.

27 Ye see, my children, how that there are two in all things, one against the other, and the one is hidden by the other: in wealth is hidden covetousness; in jovial brotherliness, drunkenness; in laughter, grief; in wedlock, reckless extravagance.

28 Death succeedeth to life, dishonour to glory, night to day, and darkness to light; and all things are under the day, just things under life, unjust things under death; wherefore also eternal life cometh only after death and much sorrow here.

29 Nor may it be said that truth is a lie, nor right wrong; for all truth is under the light, even as all things are under God.

30 All these things, therefore, I proved in my life, and I wandered not from the truth of the Lord, and I searched out the commandments of the Most High, walking according to all my strength with singleness of face unto that which is good.

The Lord would say that the secret to this life is moderation in all things physical and heeding the Holy Ghost in all things internal. Asher is saying the same more poetically.

31 Take heed, therefore, ye also, my children, to the commandments of the Lord, following the truth with singleness of face.

32 For they that are double-faced are guilty of a twofold sin; for they both do the evil thing and they have pleasure in them that do it, following the example of the spirits of deceit, and striving against mankind.

33 Do ye, therefore, my children, keep the law of the Lord, and give not heed unto evil as unto good; but look unto the thing that is really good, and keep it in all commandments of the Lord, having your conversation therein, and resting therein.

Despite all of men and women's duality now, in the end he will either be claimed by the Lord or by Satan, not both.

34 For the latter ends of men do show their righteousness or unrighteousness, when they meet the angels of the Lord and of Satan.

35 For when the soul departs troubled, it is tormented by the evil spirit which also it served in lusts and evil works.

36 But if he is peaceful with joy he meeteth the angel of peace, and he leadeth him into eternal life.

37 Become not, my children, as Sodom, which sinned against the angels of the Lord, and perished for ever.

38 For I know that ye shall sin, and be delivered into the hands of your enemies; and your land shall be made desolate, and your holy places destroyed, and ye shall be scattered unto the four corners of the earth.

39 And ye shall be set at nought in the dispersion vanishing away as water.

40 Until the Most High shall visit the earth, coming Himself as man, with men eating and drinking, and breaking the head of the dragon in the water.[38]

Feasters, remember our feast from Jonah? It is here again. Hell is in the sea.[39]

41 He shall save Israel and all the Gentiles, God speaking in the person of man.

42 Therefore do ye also, my children, tell these things to your children, that they disobey Him not.

43 For I have known that ye shall assuredly be disobedient, and assuredly act ungodly, not giving heed to the law of God, but to the commandments of men, being corrupted through wickedness.

44 And therefore shall ye be scattered as Gad and Dan my brethren, and ye shall know not your lands, tribe, and tongue.

For Asher, the holy land and the holy tongue would be lost but God would "hiss" for them and bring them home. This hissing, as the scriptures describe it, would be better translated "whispering" but it is hissing in that it is not a loud voice that calls them. Until they embrace the fullness and have access to the Holy Ghost within, the call of the shepherd is as a "hiss" in the wilderness. It is there if you are still and listen, but it is drowned out all to quickly if one is loud, drunk, amused, or overly busy. It is, however, consistent and this is why so many of the Lord's elect are gathering. It is God's mercy.

45 But the Lord will gather you together in faith through His tender mercy, and for the sake of Abraham, Isaac, and Jacob."

46 And when he had said these things unto them, he commanded them, saying: "Bury me in Hebron."

47 And he fell asleep and died at a good old age.

48 And his sons did as he had commanded them, and they carried him up to Hebron, and buried him with his fathers.

Genesis 46:17 And the sons of Asher; Jimnah, and Ishuah, and Isui, and Beriah, and Serah their sister: and the sons of Beriah; Heber, and Malchiel.

LATTER-DAY LESSONS FROM FATHER ASHER

One of the most glorious truths restored to us by the prophet Joseph is a statement between the Father and the Son at the beginning of our mortality. The Father said that the great gift of Telestial life would be the opportunity for men and women to learn the differences between good and evil by their own experience. Now, on hearing that Lucifer said, "Great, let's all sin so we can learn." This is one of the core principles taught in Mahanism. It is a satanic twisting of the truth. President Spencer W. Kimball would say that a smart man learns from the mistakes of others, and tries to do better than they did, avoiding their pitfalls. That is the recurring message of the great patriarchs of Israel. It is also reassuring to see how they matured in brotherly love and intelligence. Ultimately, Father Israel lost none of his children to Satan despite terrible sins of the worst kind. Oh, that all of us may be so fortunate in the end. The good news is that

God doesn't judge any of us until the end and so we press on while there is time to do so. President Kimball would go on to say that he did not need to step in front of a semi truck to learn that it was a bad idea. That was one in which we could wisely learn from another's poor choices. Much of life, he said, was like that. It's okay not to step in front of the truck. We can learn from the sons of Israel.

Asher warns his children of the great diaspora of their family; first the Kingdom of Israel by Assyria and second the Kingdom of Judah by Babylon.[40] All of this witnesses the words of Moses and stands as proof that the Lord God had warned the Israelites from the very beginning. If they fell away they would be thrown amid the nations. There they would become a hiss and a byword instead of a light on a hill to the world.

Father Jacob said:

Genesis 49:20 Out of Asher his bread shall be fat, and he shall yield royal dainties.

Moses added this:

Deuteronomy 33:24 ...Let Asher be blessed with children; let him be acceptable to his brethren, and let him dip his foot in oil.

25 Thy shoes shall be iron and brass; and as thy days, so shall thy strength be.

Also, it is wonderful to note that at the birth of our Lord, when his parents took him to the Temple in Jerusalem to present him there, one of the Temple matrons, called Anna the prophetess (because she was a temple matron) saw the baby Messiah and gave thanks to the Father openly. She was from the tribe of Asher.

Death of Mother Rachel at Bethlehem by Gustav Ferdinand Metz, circa 1847.

Chapter Eleven

Joseph
Zaphenath-paneah

Ye see, therefore, my children, how great things patience worketh, and prayer with fasting. So ye too, if ye follow after chastity and purity with patience and prayer, with fasting in humility of heart, the Lord will dwell among you because He loveth chastity. Love one another, and with long-suffering hide ye one another's faults. — *Joseph*

Joseph was the eleventh son of Jacob and the first son of Rachel, the beloved wife. His death bed testimony about all that he was put through from the betrayal of his own brothers to his continual struggle with his Egyptian mistress is a sad tale. The glory comes from the knowledge that Joseph, like us, will gain our crown by overcoming that which is thrust upon us.

It speaks well of Father Joseph that despite all that he was put through, he never sought revenge nor threw his sorrows back in the face of his brothers. Note also the poetry of his words. It is an entirely different word print, closer to Celestial poetry. All Israel argued that Joseph was the best of the sons of Israel. If he had any human frailties they seem to have been born of immaturity in his youth. He would be named, Joseph or *may God add upon* by his mother, in hopes of another son, but he would be renamed *Zaphenath-paneah* by his pharaonic father, a name which means: "He who is called Life." A beautiful way of saying, "Saviour." [41]

Joseph 1:1 The copy of the Testament of Joseph.

2 When he was about to die he called his sons and his brethren together, and said to them:

3 My brethren and my children, hearken to Joseph the beloved of Israel; give ear, my sons, unto your father.

4 I have seen in my life envy and death, yet I went not astray, but persevered in the truth of the Lord.

5 These my brethren hated me, but the Lord loved me:

6 They wished to slay me, but the God of my fathers guarded me:

7 They let me down into a pit, and the Most High brought me up again.

8 I was sold into slavery, and the Lord of all made me free:

9 I was taken into captivity, and His strong hand succoured me.

10 I was beset with hunger, and the Lord Himself nourished me.

11 I was alone, and God comforted me:

12 I was sick, and the Lord visited me.

13 I was in prison, and my God showed favour unto me;

14 In bonds, and He released me;

15 Slandered, and He pleaded my cause;

16 Bitterly spoken against by the Egyptians, and He delivered me;

17 Envied by my fellow-slaves, and He exalted me.[42]

18 And this chief captain of Pharaoh entrusted to me his house.

19 And I struggled against a shameless woman, urging me to transgress with her; but the God of Israel my father delivered me from the burning flame.

20 I was cast into prison, I was beaten, I was mocked; but the Lord granted me to find mercy in the sight of the keeper of the prison.

21 For the Lord doth not forsake them that fear Him, neither in darkness, nor in bonds, nor in tribulations, nor in necessities.

22 For God is not put to shame as a man, nor as the son of man is he afraid, nor as one that is earth-born is He weak or affrighted.

23 But in all those things doth He give protection, and in divers ways doth He comfort, though for a little space He departeth to try the inclination of the soul.

24 In ten temptations He showed me approved, and in all of them I endured; for endurance is a mighty charm, and patience giveth many good things.[43]

25 How often did the Egyptian woman threaten me with death!

26 How often did she give me over to punishment, and then call me back and threaten me, and when I was unwilling to company with her, she said to me:

27 Thou shalt be lord of me, and all that is in my house, if thou wilt give thyself unto me, and thou shalt be as our master.

28 But I remembered the words of my father, and going into my chamber, I wept and prayed unto the Lord.

29 And I fasted in those seven years, and I appeared to the Egyptians as one living delicately, for they that fast for God's sake receive beauty of face.[44]

30 And if my lord were away from home, I drank no wine; nor for three days did I take my food, but I gave it to the poor and sick.

31 And I sought the Lord early, and I wept for the Egyptian woman of Memphis,[45] for very unceasingly did she trouble me, for also at night she came to me under pretense of visiting me.

32 And because she had no male child she pretended to regard me as a son.

33 And for a time she embraced me as a son, and I knew it not; but later, she sought to draw me into fornication.[46]

34 And when I perceived it I sorrowed unto death; and when she had gone out, I came to myself, and lamented for her many days, because I recognized her guile and her deceit.

35 And I declared unto her the words of the Most High, in hope that she would turn from her evil lust.

36 Often, therefore, did she flatter me with words as a holy man, and guilefully in her talk praise my chastity before her husband, while desiring to ensnare me when we were alone.

37 For she lauded me openly as chaste, and in secret she said unto me: "Fear not my husband; for he is persuaded concerning thy chastity: for even should one tell him concerning us, he would not believe."

38 Owing to all these things I lay upon the ground, and besought God that the Lord would deliver me from her deceit.

39 And when she had prevailed nothing thereby, she came again to me under the plea of instruction, that she might learn the word of God.

40 And she said unto me: "If thou willest that I should leave my idols, lie with me, and I will persuade my husband to depart from his idols, and we will walk in the law by thy Lord."

41 And I said unto her: "The Lord willeth not that those who reverence Him should be in uncleanness, nor doth He take pleasure in them that commit adultery, but in those that approach Him with a pure heart and undefiled lips."

42 But she bided her time, longing to accomplish her evil desire with me.

43 And I gave myself yet more to fasting and prayer, that the Lord might deliver me from her.

44 And again, at another time she said unto me: "If thou wilt not commit adultery, I will kill my husband by poison; and take thee to be my husband."

45 I therefore, when I heard this, rent my garments, and said unto her:

46 "Woman, reverence God, and do not this evil deed, lest thou be destroyed; for know indeed that I will declare this thy device unto all men."

47 She therefore, being afraid, besought that I would not declare this device.

48 And she departed soothing me with gifts, and sending to me every delight of the sons of men.

49 And afterwards she sent me food mingled with enchantments.

50 And when the eunuch who brought it came, I looked up and beheld a terrible man giving me with the dish a sword, and I perceived that her scheme was to beguile me.

51 And when he had gone out I wept, nor did I taste that or any other of her food.

52 So then after one day she came to me and observed the food, and said unto me: "Why is it that thou hast not eaten of the food?"

53 And I said unto her: "It is because thou hast filled it with deadly enchantments; and how saidst thou: 'I come not near to idols but to the Lord alone.'

54 Now therefore know that the God of my father hath revealed unto me by His angel thy wickedness, and I have kept it to convict thee, in the hope that thou mayst see and repent.

55 But that thou mayst learn that the wickedness of the ungodly hath no power over them that worship God with chastity behold I will take of it and eat before thee."

56 And having so said, I prayed thus: "The God of my fathers and the angel of Abraham, be with me;" and I ate in front of her.

57 And when she saw this she fell upon her face at my feet, weeping; and I raised her up and admonished her.

58 And she promised to do this iniquity no more.

59 But her heart was still set upon evil, and she looked around how to ensnare me, and sighing deeply she became downcast, though she was not sick.

60 And when her husband saw her, he said unto her: "Why is thy countenance fallen?"

61 And she said unto him: "I have a pain at my heart, and the groanings of my spirit oppress me;" and so he comforted her who was not sick.

62 Then, accordingly seizing an opportunity, she rushed unto me while her husband was yet without, and said unto me: "I will hang myself, or cast myself over a cliff, if thou wilt not lie with me."

63 And when I saw the spirit of Beliar was troubling her, I prayed unto the Lord, and said unto her:

64 "Why, wretched woman, art thou troubled and disturbed, blinded through sins?

65 Remember that if thou kill thyself, Asteho, the concubine of thy husband, thy rival, will beat thy children, and thou wilt destroy thy memorial from off the earth."

66 And she said unto me: "Lo, then thou lovest me; let this suffice me: only strive for my life and my children, and I expect that I shall enjoy my desire also."

67 But she knew not that I said this out of pity for her husband, my master, and not because of her.

68 For if a man hath fallen before the passion of a wicked desire and become enslaved by it, even as she, whatever good thing he may hear with regard to that passion, he receiveth it with a view to his wicked desire.

69 I declare, therefore, unto you, my children, that it was about the sixth hour when she departed from me; and I knelt before the Lord all day, and all the

night; and about dawn I rose up, weeping the while and praying for a release from her.

70 At last, then, she laid hold of my garments, forcibly dragging me to have connexion with her.

71 When, therefore, I saw that in her madness she was holding fast to my garment, I left it behind, and fled away naked.

72 And holding fast to the garment she falsely accused me, and when her husband came he cast me into prison in his house; and on the morrow he scourged me and sent me into Pharaoh's prison.

73 And when I was in bonds, the Egyptian woman was oppressed with grief, and she came and heard how I gave thanks unto the Lord and sang praises in the abode of darkness, and with glad voice rejoiced, glorifying my God that I was delivered from the lustful desire of that Egyptian woman.

74 And often hath she sent unto me saying: Consent to fulfil my desire, and I will release thee from thy bonds, and I will free thee from the darkness.

75 And not even in thought did I incline unto her.

76 For God loveth him who in a den of wickedness combines fasting with chastity, rather than the man who in kings' chambers combines luxury with license.

77 And if a man liveth in chastity, and desireth also glory, and the Most High knoweth that it is expedient for him, He bestoweth this also upon him.

78 How often, though she were sick, did she come down to me at unlooked for times, and listened to my voice as I prayed!

79 And when I heard her groanings I held my peace.

80 For when I was in her house she was wont to bare her arms, and breasts, and legs, that I might lie with her; for she was very beautiful, splendidly adorned in order to beguile me.

81 And the Lord guarded me from her devices.

If any man had the opportunity to fall in this life it was Joseph and yet he did not.

Joseph 2:1 Ye see, therefore, my children, how great things patience worketh, and prayer with fasting.

2 So ye too, if ye follow after chastity and purity with patience and prayer, with fasting in humility of heart, the Lord will dwell among you because He loveth chastity.

3 And wheresoever the Most High dwelleth, even though envy, or slavery, or slander befalleth a man, the Lord who dwelleth in him, for the sake of his chastity not only delivereth him from evil, but also exalteth him even as me.

4 For in every way the man is lifted up, whether in deed, or in word, or in thought.

This next section shows Joseph's inner-mind in regard to the events of his life. His brothers would probably not agree exactly with Joseph's perspective. They saw Joseph as over-coddled, favored, and spoiled. Joseph is here saying that despite everything that happened, his intent was never evil. I actually think both realities are true. I think that Joseph didn't understand how hard the greater family dynamic had been on everyone. I also think that he was immature at the time he was sold but truly didn't have any evil intentions.

5 My brethren knew how my father loved me, and yet I did not exalt myself in my mind: although I was a child, I had the fear of God in my heart; for I knew that all things would pass away.

6 And I did not raise myself against them with evil intent, but I honoured my brethren; and out of respect for them, even when I was being sold, I refrained from telling the Ishmaelites that I was a son of Jacob, a great man and a mighty.

7 Do ye also, my children, have the fear of God in all your works before your eyes, and honour your brethren.

8 For every one who doeth the law of the Lord shall be loved by Him.

9 And when I came to the Indocolpitae with the Ishmaelites, they asked me, saying:

10 "Art thou a slave?" And I said that I was a home-born slave, that I might not put my brethren to shame.

11 And the eldest of them said unto me: Thou art not a slave, for even thy appearance doth make it manifest [that thou art a free man's son.]

12 But I said that I was their slave.

13 Now when we came into Egypt they strove concerning me, which of them should buy me and take me.

14 Therefore it seemed good to all that I should remain in Egypt with the merchant of their trade, until they should return bringing merchandise.

15 And the Lord gave me favour in the eyes of the merchant, and he entrusted unto me his house.

16 And God blessed him by my means, and increased him in gold and silver and in household servants.

17 And I was with him three months and five days.

18 And about that time the Memphian woman, the wife of Pentephris came down in a chariot, with great pomp, because she had heard from her eunuchs concerning me.

19 And she told her husband that the merchant had become rich by means of a young Hebrew, and, "They say that he had assuredly been stolen out of the land of Canaan.

20 Now, therefore, render justice unto him, and take away the youth to thy house; so shall the God of the Hebrews bless thee, for grace from heaven is upon him."

21 And Pentephris was persuaded by her words, and commanded the merchant to be brought, and said unto him:

22 "What is this that I hear concerning thee, that thou stealest persons out of the land of Canaan, and sellest them for slaves?"

23 But the merchant fell at his feet, and besought him, saying: "I beseech thee, my lord, I know not what thou sayest."

24 And Pentephris said unto him: "Whence, then, is the Hebrew slave?"

25 And he said: "The Ishmaelites entrusted him unto me until they should return."

26 But he believed him not, but commanded him to be stripped and beaten.

27 And when he persisted in this statement, Pentephris said: "Let the youth be brought."

28 And when I was brought in, I did obeisance to Pentephris for he was third in rank of the officers of Pharaoh.

29 And he took me apart from him, and said unto me: "Art thou a slave or free?"

30 And I said: "A slave."

31 And he said: "Whose?"

32 And I said: "The Ishmaelites'."

33 And he said: "How didst thou become their slave?"

34 And I said: "They bought me out of the land of Canaan."

35 And he said unto me: "Truly thou liest;" and straightway he commanded me to be stripped and beaten.

36 Now, the Memphian woman was looking through a window at me while I was being beaten, for her house was near, and she sent unto him saying:

37 "Thy judgement is unjust; for thou dost punish a free man who hath been stolen, as though he were a transgressor."

38 And when I made no change in my statement, though I was beaten, he ordered me to be imprisoned, until, he said, the owners of the boy should come.

39 And the woman said unto her husband: "Wherefore dost thou detain the captive and wellborn lad in bonds, who ought rather to be set at liberty, and be waited upon?"

40 For she wished to see me out of a desire of sin, but I was ignorant concerning all these things at that time.

41 And he said to her: "It is not the custom of the Egyptians to take that which belongeth to others before proof is given."

42 This, therefore, he said concerning the merchant; but as for the lad, he must be imprisoned.

43 Now after four and twenty days came the Ishmaelites; for they had heard that Jacob my father was mourning much concerning me.

44 And they came and said unto me: "How is it that thou saidst that thou wast a slave? and lo, we have learnt that thou art the son of a mighty man in the land of Canaan, and thy father still mourneth for thee in sackcloth and ashes."

45 When I heard this my bowels were dissolved and my heart melted, and I desired greatly to weep, but I restrained myself that I should not put my brethren to shame.

46 And I said unto them, "I know not, I am a slave."

47 Then, therefore, they took counsel to sell me, that I should not be found in their hands.

48 For they feared my father, lest he should come and execute upon them a grievous vengeance.

49 For they had heard that he was mighty with God and with men.

50 Then said the merchant unto them: "Release me from the judgement of Pentiphri."

51 And they came and requested me, saying: "Say that thou wast bought by us with money, and he will set us free."

52 Now the Memphian woman said to her husband: "Buy the youth; for I hear," said she, "that they are selling him."

53 And straightway she sent a eunuch to the Ishmaelites, and asked them to sell me.

54 But since the eunuch would not agree to buy me at their price he returned, having made trial of them, and he made known to his mistress that they asked a large price for their slave.

55 And she sent another eunuch, saying: "Even though they demand two minas, give them, do not spare the gold; only buy the boy, and bring him to me."

56 The eunuch therefore went and gave them eighty pieces of gold, and he received me; but to the Egyptian woman he said I have given a hundred.

57 And though I knew this I held my peace, lest the eunuch should be put to shame.

58 Ye see, therefore, my children, what great things I endured that I should not put my brethren to shame.

59 Do ye also, therefore, love one another, and with long-suffering hide ye one another's faults.[47]

60 For God delighteth in the unity of brethren, and in the purpose of a heart that takes pleasure in love.

61 And when my brethren came into Egypt they learnt that I had returned their money unto them, and upbraided them not, and comforted them.

62 And after the death of Jacob my father I loved them more abundantly, and all things whatsoever he commanded I did very abundantly for them.

63 And I suffered them not to be afflicted in the smallest matter; and all that was in my hand I gave unto them.

64 And their children were my children, and my children as their servants; and their life was my life, and all their suffering was my suffering, and all their sickness was my infirmity.

65 My land was their land, and their counsel my counsel.

66 And I exalted not myself among them in arrogance because of my worldly glory, but I was among them as one of the least.

67 If ye also, therefore, walk in the commandments of the Lord, my children, He will exalt you there, and will bless you with good things for ever and ever.

68 And if any one seeketh to do evil unto you, do well unto him, and pray for him, and ye shall be redeemed of the Lord from all evil.

69 For, behold, ye see that out of my humility and longsuffering I took unto wife the daughter of the priest of Heliopolis.

70 And a hundred talents of gold were given me with her, and the Lord made them to serve me.

71 And He gave me also beauty as a flower beyond the beautiful ones of Israel; and He preserved me unto old age in strength and in beauty, because I was like in all things to Jacob.

72 And hear ye, my children, also the vision which I saw.

73 There were twelve harts feeding: and the nine were first dispersed over all the earth, and likewise also the three.

74 And I saw that from Judah was born a virgin wearing a linen garment, and from her, was born a lamb, without spot; and on his left hand there was as it were a lion; and all the beasts rushed against him, and the lamb overcame them, and destroyed them and trod them under foot.

75 And because of him the angels and men rejoiced, and all the land.

76 And these things shall come to pass in their season, in the last days.

77 Do ye therefore, my children, observe the commandments of the Lord, and honour Levi and Judah; for from them shall arise unto you the Lamb of God, who taketh away the sin of the world, one who saveth all the Gentiles and Israel.

78 For His kingdom is an everlasting kingdom, which shall not pass away; but my kingdom among you shall come to an end as a watcher's hammock, which after the summer disappeareth.

79 For I know that after my death the Egyptians will afflict you, but God will avenge you, and will bring you into that which He promised to your fathers.

80 But ye shall carry up my bones with you; for when my bones are being taken up thither, the Lord shall be with you in light, and Beliar shall be in darkness with the Egyptians.

81 And carry ye up Asenath your mother to the *family tomb*, and near Rachel your mother bury her.[48]

82 And when he had said these things he stretched out his feet, and died at a good old age.

83 And all Israel mourned for him, and all Egypt, with a great mourning.

84 And when the children of Israel went out of Egypt, they took with them the bones of Joseph, and they buried him in Hebron with his fathers, and the years of his life were one hundred and ten years.

Genesis 46:20 And unto Joseph in the land of Egypt were born Manasseh and Ephraim, which Asenath the daughter of Poti-pherah priest of On bare unto him.

LATTER-DAY LESSONS FROM FATHER JOSEPH

We Gospel Feasters of the Latter-days hold an especially fond place in our hearts for Joseph. He is the father of the vast majority of the Saints who make up the Body of Christ in the Latter-days. He was far and beyond the most righteous of all of Israel's sons and was in fact their under-shepherd and Saviour on Mount Zion. His testimony adds tremendous weight to his mission, sorrow and humanity. Even the Jews hold him in great awe and acknowledge that he was the best son of Israel; better than their father Judah; who did in the end grow up.

Mormons also have this restored pearl which shows that Joseph's seership was greater than even the few remnants we have of him:

JST Genesis 50:24 And Joseph said unto his brethren, I die, and go unto my fathers; and I go down to my grave with joy. The God of my father Jacob be with you, to deliver you out of affliction in the days of your bondage; for the Lord hath visited me, and I have obtained a promise of the Lord, that out of the fruit of my loins, the Lord God will raise up a righteous branch out of my loins; and unto thee, whom my father Jacob hath named Israel, a prophet; (not the Messiah who is called Shilo); and this prophet shall deliver my people out of Egypt in the days of thy bondage.

Unless this is speaking of Joshua – and it probably is – this is saying that Moses was also a descendant of Joseph in some manner we do not understand. Perhaps one of his grandmothers was a daughter of Ephraim or Manasseh.

25 And it shall come to pass that they shall be scattered again; and a branch shall be broken off, and shall be carried into a far country; nevertheless they shall be remembered in the covenants of the Lord, when the Messiah cometh; for he shall be made manifest unto them in the latter days, in the Spirit of power; and shall bring them out of darkness into light; out of hidden darkness, and out of captivity unto freedom.

We know the names of these of our kin, the Nephites and the Lamanites and all the great tribes called today Native American. Their heritage is the Book of Momon and their parents are some of the greatest of the prophets.

26 A seer shall the Lord my God raise up, who shall be a choice seer unto the fruit of my loins.

27 Thus saith the Lord God of my fathers unto me, A choice seer will I raise up out of the fruit of thy loins, and he shall be esteemed highly among the fruit of thy loins; and unto him will I give commandment that he shall do a work for the fruit of thy loins, his brethren.

28 And he shall bring them to the knowledge of the covenants which I have made with thy fathers; and he shall do whatsoever work I shall command him.

29 And I will make him great in mine eyes, for he shall do my work; and he shall be great like unto him whom I have said I would raise up unto you, to deliver my people, O house of Israel, out of the land of Egypt; for a seer will I raise up to deliver my people out of the land of Egypt; and he shall be called Moses. And by this name he shall know that he is of thy house; for he shall be nursed by the king's daughter, and shall be called her son.

This is Joseph Smith, Jr. our prophet and seer. The Lord would call him great, as Moses was great. Joseph Smith bears the honor of being one of only seven dispensational patriarchs; one of which was Moses.

30 And again, a seer will I raise up out of the fruit of thy loins, and unto him will I give power to bring forth my word unto the seed of thy loins; and not to the bringing forth of my word only, saith the Lord, but to the convincing them of my word, which shall have already gone forth among them in the last days;

31 Wherefore the fruit of thy loins shall write, and the fruit of the loins of Judah shall write; and that which shall be written by the fruit of thy loins, and also that which shall be written by the fruit of the loins of Judah, shall grow together unto the confounding of false doctrines, and laying down of contentions, and establishing peace among the fruit of thy loins, and bringing them to a knowledge of their fathers in the latter days; and also to the knowledge of my covenants, saith the Lord.[49]

32 And out of weakness shall he be made strong, in that day when my work shall go forth among all my people, which shall restore them, who are of the house of Israel, in the last days.

33 And that seer will I bless, and they that seek to destroy him shall be confounded; for this promise I give unto you; for I will remember you from generation to generation; and his name shall be called Joseph, and it shall be after the name of his father; and he shall be like unto you; for the thing which the Lord shall bring forth by his hand shall bring my people unto salvation.

34 And the Lord sware unto Joseph that he would preserve his seed forever, saying, I will raise up Moses, and a rod shall be in his hand, and he shall gather together my people, and he shall lead them as a flock, and he shall smite the waters of the Red Sea with his rod.

35 And he shall have judgment, and shall write the word of the Lord. And he shall not speak many words, for I will write unto him my law by the finger of mine own hand. And I will make a spokesman for him, and his name shall be called Aaron.

36 And it shall be done unto thee in the last days also, even as I have sworn. Therefore, Joseph said unto his brethren, God will surely visit you, and bring you out of this land, unto the land which he sware unto Abraham, and unto Isaac, and to Jacob.

37 And Joseph confirmed many other things unto his brethren, and took an oath of the children of Israel, saying unto them, God will surely visit you, and ye shall carry up my bones from hence.

Mark it yet again: Salvation, in part anyway, is defined as having place and inheritance on Holy Land, specifically within the "House of God."

38 So Joseph died when he was an hundred and ten years old; and they embalmed him, and they put him in a coffin in Egypt; and he was kept from burial by the children of Israel, that he might be carried up and laid in the sepulchre with his father. And thus they remembered the oath which they sware unto him.

Joseph received the greatest blessings of both Israel & Moses. We of the church today are grateful because it is these blessings that are sustaining our efforts to prepare the Earth for the second coming. We have no help in this as a tribe but the promises of our fathers and the arm of Jesus Christ; thus it is enough, if we will just keep at it. First Israel:

Genesis 49:22 Joseph is a fruitful bough, even a fruitful bough by a well; whose branches run over the wall:

23 The archers have sorely grieved him, and shot at him, and hated him:

24 But his bow abode in strength, and the arms of his hands were made strong by the hands of the mighty God of Jacob; (from thence is the shepherd, the stone of Israel:)

25 Even by the God of thy father, who shall help thee; and by the Almighty, who shall bless thee with blessings of heaven above, blessings of the deep that lieth under, blessings of the breasts, and of the womb:

26 The blessings of thy father have prevailed above the blessings of my progenitors unto the utmost bound of the everlasting hills: they shall be on the head of Joseph, and on the crown of the head of him that was separate from his brethren.

And Moses:

Deuteronomy 33: 13 And of Joseph he said, Blessed of the Lord be his land, for the precious things of heaven, for the dew, and for the deep that coucheth beneath,

14 And for the precious fruits brought forth by the sun, and for the precious things put forth by the moon,

15 And for the chief things of the ancient mountains, and for the precious things of the lasting hills,

16 And for the precious things of the earth and fulness thereof, and for the good will of him that dwelt in the bush: let the blessing come upon the head of Joseph, and upon the top of the head of him that was separated from his brethren.

17 His glory is like the firstling of his bullock, and his horns are like the horns of unicorns: with them he shall push the people together to the ends of the earth: and they are the ten thousands of Ephraim, and they are the thousands of Manasseh.

I take deep pride in being a son of Joseph, a pharaoh[50] of Egypt, via his son Ephraim. He was chosen ultimately to be separated from his family in order to save them by carving out a Zion space in the heart of Babylon. His calling then is our calling now. Our Father Joseph was the ultimate saviour on Mount Zion. He is the model of our actions now in the Restoration. Joseph as a bull pushed his family to a safe pasture and then guarded them there by the holy priesthood and as a powerful seer.

His wife, the beautiful Asenath became the desert-Zion, the Queen Bee of the hive or gathering and the sweet labour of honey. Our latter-day sisters, the daughters of Zion fill her role in making our desert Zion sweet and glorious. As we have discussed at length in the *Gospel Feast Series*, it is the male priesthood which builds a zone of safety so that the feminine spirit can feather the nest of happiness within. When these two forces work in harmony, the happiness that is created make the angels smile, the devil furious and the saints celestial.

We don't know as much about Asenath as we would like too. What we do know is that she was strikingly beautiful, humble and the love of Joseph's life. We know she bore at least 2 sons and there is rumor of a possible daughter. When she embraced the God of her husband, she was blessed and sanctified as a Lady Zion, a holy space of refuge in the wilderness of the world.[51] Egypt in the days of the first Joseph and the lands of Deseret in the Latter-days. It was also another sign to the faithful that the Restored Gospel is true. That Joseph Smith was a true prophet and that God's power has indeed been restored to the Earth.

The Grain Distribution Center at Saqqara Egypt build by Father Joseph the vice-pharaoh. See *Genesis part 4* for more information.

Joseph Reunited with His Brothers (especially Benjamin whom he's hugging) by
Léon Pierre Urbain Bourgeois, oil on canvas, at the Musée Municipal Frédéric
Blandin, Nevers, 1863.

Chapter Twelve

Benjamin

For as the sun is not defiled by shining on dung and mire, but rather drieth up both and driveth away the evil smell; so also the pure mind, though encompassed by the defilements of earth, rather cleanseth them and is not itself defiled. - Benjamin

Benjamin was the twelfth son of Jacob and Rachel, the baby of the family. From his testimony it is clear that he was both a philosopher and philanthropist. He would have been 5 years old when his only full brother Joseph "disappeared" from the family.

Benjamin 1:1 The copy of the words of Benjamin, which he commanded his sons to observe, after he had lived a hundred and twenty-five years.

2 And he kissed them, and said: "As Isaac was born to Abraham in his old age, so also was I to Jacob.

3 And since Rachel my mother died in giving me birth, I had no milk; therefore I was suckled by Bilhah her handmaid.[52]

4 For Rachel remained barren for twelve years after she had borne Joseph; and she prayed to the Lord with fasting twelve days, and she conceived and bare me.

5 For my father loved Rachel dearly, and prayed that he might see two sons born from her.

6 Therefore was I called Benjamin, that is, a son of days.[53]

7 And when I went into Egypt, to Joseph, and my brother recognized me, he said unto me: "What did they tell my father when they sold me?"

All those years of wondering. Think of it? Poor Joseph.

8 And I said unto him, "They dabbled thy coat with blood and sent it, and said: Know whether this be thy son's coat?"

9 And he said unto me: "Even so, brother, when they had stripped me of my coat they gave me to the Ishmaelites, who gave me a loin cloth, scourged me, and bade me run alongside them.

10 And as for one of them that had beaten me with a rod, a lion met him and slew him.

11 And so his associates were afraid to hurt me."

Again note the detail of the story. You will remember that Joseph's guilty brothers said they took Joseph's fine clothes and dressed him as a slave, so as to better conform him to their story at his sale. It is dangerous to steal, buy or mistreat a prince. His father, a king, may just want him back. It is permitted in the laws of heaven for a man to defend, even to death, his wife and children. It is dangerous to offend a powerful man. Had Joseph been dressed as a prince, the Ishmaelites would never have bought him. Joseph's brothers said, "His a slave. See, he is dressed as a slave." Joseph gives us the bigger truth, they stripped him nude, and sold him. Joseph learned pretty quickly that complaining and crying would only get him beat by his new masters.[54]

12 Do ye also, therefore, my children, love the Lord God of heaven and earth, and keep His commandments, following the example of the good and holy man Joseph.

13 And let your mind be unto good, even as ye know me; for he that hath his mind right seeth all things rightly.

14 Fear ye the Lord, and love your neighbour; and even though the spirits of Beliar claim you to afflict you with every evil, yet shall they not have dominion over you, even as they had not over Joseph my brother.

15 How many men wished to slay Joseph! And God shielded him!

16 For he that feareth God and loveth his neighbour cannot be smitten by the spirit of Beliar, being shielded by the fear of God.

This is why Satan will get a man drunk before his rage. The fear of the Lord is weakened by drugs and intoxication.

17 Nor can he be ruled over by the device of men or beasts, for he is helped by the Lord through the love which he hath towards his neighbour.

18 For Joseph also besought our father that he would pray for his brethren, that the Lord would not impute to them as sin whatever evil they had done unto him.

19 And thus Jacob cried out: "My good child, thou hast prevailed over the bowels of thy father Jacob."

It was Joseph who curbed what might have been his father's rage. Noah brought a curse upon Ham and Canaan when he was enraged by his family's bad actions. Curses by a righteous patriarch are binding and difficult to undo. Had Israel chosen to curse some or all of his sons for their evil, the ramifications could have been eternal. Joseph did what Jesus Christ would later do: asked his father to forgive all the offenses brought upon him by his family. Israel knew what it meant, check this out:

Benjamin 1:20 And Jacob embraced Joseph, and kissed him for two hours, saying:

Two hours? Jacob really did love Joseph.

21 "In thee shall be fulfilled the prophecy of heaven concerning the Lamb of God, and Saviour of the world, and that a blameless one shall be delivered up for lawless men, and a sinless one shall die for ungodly men in the blood of the covenant, for the salvation of the Gentiles and of Israel, and shall destroy Beliar and his servants."

22 See ye, therefore, my children, the end of the good man?

In other words, the Lord Jesus Christ was seen in the life and perseverance of Joseph. To this date, no one had walked the earth who better typified all the Lord would do than Joseph.[55]

23 Be followers of his compassion, therefore, with a good mind, that ye also may wear crowns of glory.

24 For the good man hath not a dark eye; for he showeth mercy to all men, even though they be sinners.

25 And though they devise with evil intent concerning him, by doing good he overcometh evil, being shielded by God; and he loveth the righteous as his own soul.

26 If any one is glorified, he envieth him not; if any one is enriched, he is not jealous; if any one is valiant, he praiseth him; the virtuous man he laudeth; on the poor man he hath mercy; on the weak he hath compassion; unto God he singeth praises.

27 And him that hath the grace of a good spirit he loveth as his own soul.

28 If therefore, ye also have a good mind, then will both wicked men be at peace with you, and the recklessly extravagant will reverence you and turn to your good; and the covetous will not only cease from their inordinate desire, but even give the objects of their covetousness to them that are afflicted.

29 If ye do well, even the unclean spirits will flee from you; and the beasts will dread you.

30 For where there is reverence for good works and light in the mind, even darkness fleeth away from him.

31 For if any one does violence to a holy man, he repenteth; for the holy man is merciful to his reviler, and holdeth his peace.

32 And if any one betrayeth a righteous man, the righteous man prayeth: though for a little he be humbled, yet not long after he appeareth far more glorious, as was Joseph my brother.

33 The inclination of the good man is not in the power of the deceit of the spirit of Beliar, for the angel of peace guideth his soul.

34 And he gazeth not passionately upon corruptible things, nor gathereth together riches through a desire of pleasure.

35 He delighteth not in pleasure, he grieveth not his neighbour, he sateth not himself with luxuries, he erreth not in the uplifting of the eyes, for the Lord is his portion.

36 The good inclination receiveth not glory nor dishonour from men, and it knoweth not any guile, or lie, or fighting or reviling; for the Lord dwelleth in him and lighteth up his soul, and he rejoiceth towards all men always.

37 The good mind hath not two tongues, of blessing and of cursing, of contumely and of honour, of sorrow and of joy, of quietness and of confusion, of hypocrisy and of truth, of poverty and of wealth; but it hath one disposition, uncorrupt and pure, concerning all men.

38 It hath no double sight, nor double hearing; for in everything which he doeth, or speaketh, or seeth, he knoweth that the Lord looketh on his soul.

39 And he cleanseth his mind that he may not be condemned by men as well as by God.

40 And in like manner the works of Beliar are twofold, and there is no singleness in them.[56]

41 Therefore, my children, I tell you, flee the malice of Beliar; for he giveth a sword to them that obey him.

42 And the sword is the mother of seven evils. First the mind conceiveth through Beliar, and first there is bloodshed; secondly ruin; thirdly, tribulation; fourthly, exile; fifthly, dearth; sixthly, panic; seventhly, destruction.

43 'Therefore was Cain also delivered over to seven vengeances by God, for in every hundred years the Lord brought an additional plague upon him.

44 And when he was two hundred years old he began to suffer, and in the nine-hundredth year he was destroyed.

45 For on account of Abel, his brother, with all the evils was he judged, but Lamech with seventy times seven.

46 Because for ever those, who are like Cain in envy and hatred of brethren, shall be punished with the same judgement.

Benjamin 2:1 And do ye, my children, flee evil-doing, envy, and hatred of brethren, and cleave to goodness and love.

2 He that hath a pure mind in love, looketh not after a woman with a view to fornication; for he hath no defilement in his heart, because the Spirit of God resteth upon him.

This next verse has been shown as an illustration of the "homeliness, yet vividness of the figures of speech and the intelligence of the mind of these ancient patriarchs." Modern man is arrogant to assume that his ancestors thought no deep thoughts nor created no works of art or beauty. The same level of intelligence that flows through us, flowed through our ancestors.

3 For as the sun is not defiled by shining on dung and mire, but rather drieth up both and driveth away the evil smell; so also the pure mind, though

encompassed by the defilements of earth, rather cleanseth them and is not itself defiled.

4 And I believe that there will be also evil-doings among you, from the words of Enoch the righteous: that ye shall commit fornication with the fornication of Sodom, and shall perish, all save a few, and shall renew wanton deeds with women; and the kingdom of the Lord shall not be among you, for straightway He shall take it away.

5 Nevertheless the temple of God shall be in your portion, and the last temple shall be more glorious than the first.

Jerusalem, the city and temple mount, did fall into Benjamin's allotment of land in Israel. The Benjaminites did become so wicked that the rest of the tribes nearly eradicated them, and would have except for the fact that they didn't want to ever erase another brother out of Israel like they had tried to do to Joseph.

6 And the twelve tribes shall be gathered together there, and all the Gentiles, until the Most High shall send forth His salvation in the visitation of an only-begotten prophet.[57]

7 And He shall enter into the temple, and there shall the Lord be treated with outrage, and He shall be lifted up upon a tree.

8 And the veil of the temple shall be rent, and the Spirit of God shall pass on to the Gentiles as fire poured forth.

9 And He shall ascend from the grave of death and shall pass from earth into heaven.

10 And I know how lowly He shall be on earth, and how glorious He will be in heaven.

This is an astounding prophecy for the ancients to have had, but it verifies Joseph Smith's teaching that the ancients knew the gospel.

11 Now when Joseph was in Egypt, I longed to see his figure and the form of his countenance; and through the prayers of Jacob my father I saw him, while awake in the daytime, even his entire figure exactly as he was.

12 And when Benjamin had said these things, he said to his sons: "Know ye, therefore, my children, that I am dying.

13 Act in truth each one to his neighbour, and keep the law of the Lord and His commandments.

14 For these things do I leave you instead of inheritance.

15 Teach them by word and example to your children for an everlasting possession; for so did both Abraham, and Isaac, and Jacob.

16 For all these things they gave us for an inheritance, saying: "Keep the commandments of God, until the Lord shall reveal His salvation to all Gentiles.

17 And then shall ye see Enoch, Noah, and Shem, and Abraham, and Isaac, and Jacob, rising on the right hand in gladness,

18 Then shall we also rise, each one over our tribe, worshipping the King of Heaven, who appeared upon earth in the form of a man in humility.

19 And as many as believe on Him on the earth shall rejoice with Him.

20 Then also all men shall rise, some unto glory and some unto shame.

21 And the Lord shall judge Israel first, for their unrighteousness; for when He appeared as God in the flesh to deliver them they believed Him not.

22 And then shall He judge all the Gentiles, as many as believed Him not when He appeared upon earth.

23 And He shall punish Israel through the Gentiles of His chosing, even as He reproved Esau through the Midianites, who deceived their brethren, so that they fell into fornication, and idolatry; and they were alienated from God, not having a portion with the children of them that fear the Lord.

24 If ye therefore, my children, walk in holiness according to the commandments of the Lord, ye shall again dwell securely with me, and all Israel shall be gathered unto the Lord.

25 And I shall no longer be called a ravening wolf on account of your ravages, but a worker of the Lord distributing food to them that work what is good.

Benjamin knew that his family name would stink for a time in Israel, but he always knew that, as for himself, he had received his calling and election made sure. Here he is saying that in time his tribal name would be venerated.

26 And there shall arise in time one beloved of the Lord, of our tribe, a doer of His good pleasure in his mouth, with new knowledge enlightening the Gentiles.

27 Until the consummation of the age shall he be in the synagogues of the Gentiles, and among their rulers, as a strain of music in the mouth of all.

28 And he shall be inscribed in the holy books, both his work and his word, and he shall be a chosen one of God forever.

29 And through them he shall go to and fro as Jacob my father, saying: 'He shall fill up that which lacketh of thy tribe.'"

Saul of Tarsus, perhaps the most famous of all of Benjamin's descendants would have known this and reflected on it. When he finally came to understand it, it gave him peace. Paul's expounding of the scriptures of yore, did indeed become the legacy of Benjamin. This would be the Apostle Paul, the great author of the majority of the *New Testament* as it stands today.

30 And when he had said these things he stretched out his feet.

31 And died in a beautiful and good sleep.

32 And his sons did as he had enjoined them, and they took up his body and buried it in Hebron with his fathers.

33 And the number of the days of his life was a hundred and twenty-five years.

Genesis 46:21 And the sons of Benjamin were Belah, and Becher, and Ashbel, Gera, and Naaman, Ehi, and Rosh, Muppim, and Huppim, and Ard.

22 These are the sons of Rachel, which were born to Jacob: all the souls were fourteen.

SUMMATION

Benjamin's testimony of the Messiah may be the most illuminating of all those preserved by a direct son of Israel.

Benjamin told his children to watch for a sinless man to be put to death by evil ones. He rejoiced that the future temple would sit on land held by his tribe but that it would come to an end with the death of the Messiah. Daniel would echo this exact truth in later years. He foresees the rending of the temple veil at the crucifixion as well. He adds his promise of a coming resurrection and rejoices that one of his future sons, Saul of Tarsus, renamed by the Lord Paul the Apostle, would be a Benjaminite by birth.

Father Israel left this blessing for the baby of the family:

Genesis 49:27 Benjamin shall ravin as a wolf: in the morning he shall devour the prey, and at night he shall divide the spoil.

Moses added this blessing:

Deuteronomy 33:12 ...The beloved of the Lord shall dwell in safety by him; and the Lord shall cover him all the day long, and he shall dwell between his shoulders.

The Lord Jesus Christ did perform much of His ministry in the portion of land given to Benjamin. This is one of the signs of the true Messiah which Moses left us; He would bear His burden on Benjamin's land at both Gethsemane and Calvary.

Jacob Blessing Ephraim and Manasseh by Benjamin West.

Chapter Thirteen

Ephraim & Manasseh

These sons are mine. — *Father Israel*

Our Jewish brethren have preserved for us a handful of interesting tidbits about Ephraim and Manasseh which we, their descendants, would otherwise not have.[58]

The Jews say that they were both towering men, very handsome like their father and very well built. Manasseh was particularly strong and served frequently as his father's bodyguard. It is said that he could drop a man with a single punch. One can't help but think of the mighty Polynesian houses which the *Book of Mormon* says descended from him as examples of such strength. Manasseh spoke fluent Egyptian but had been taught the ways of his fathers. He was very interested in civil matters and wanted to work in Egyptian government. As it turns out, Ephraim was much more interested in connecting with his grandfather and uncles, and being Hebrew. He petitioned his father to leave the family house for a season and go and study Hebrew at his grandfather's feet in Goshen. It is said that Father Israel took much joy in Ephraim, and in some small way, it was like having Joseph home again.

It is entirely possible that Israel's act of raising Ephraim over Manasseh, in terms of the birthright (although note they were blessed together) was in many ways the righting of the wrongs between Esau and Jacob so many years before. Esau and Jacob shared one womb and should have shared in the glorious blessings of Isaac, but Satan got into the heart of Esau and destroyed him. Ephraim and Manasseh were brothers who worked together and are still working together to build up the kingdom on this the American Continent, where their joint birthright blessings have given them the inheritance of Fathers Adam and Enoch, the very New Jerusalem. It is said that while Manasseh would shoulder the labour of physical building, the job of gathering and preparing (as Father Joseph did) would fall on Ephraim. The sign of their labour on behalf of the greater family is the ox. The same that surrounds our modern baptismal fonts. It has been whispered, but I am unaware of any authoritative declaration, that when the day comes for the building of the New Jerusalem on the site of Eden, after the American Midwest has been cleansed at the start of the Millennium, that it will be the children of Manasseh from the south that will rise up in strength to get the job done. It will be their gift to the family. The children of Lehi can be very dedicated and hardworking when they believe in a cause. When the Lord calls them, it will be cause enough to get to work.

Here is a pearl from Joseph Smith in regards to Israel's remarkable blessing:

JST, Genesis 48:5 And now, of thy two sons, Ephraim and Manasseh, which were born unto thee in the land of Egypt, before I came unto thee into Egypt; behold, they are mine, and the God of my fathers shall bless them; even as Reuben and Simeon they shall be blessed, for they are mine; wherefore they shall be called after my name. (Therefore they were called Israel.)

6 And thy issue which thou begettest after them, shall be thine, and shall be called after the name of their brethren in their inheritance, in the tribes; therefore they were called the tribes of Manasseh and of Ephraim.

7 And Jacob said unto Joseph, When the God of my fathers appeared unto me in Luz, in the land of Canaan; he sware unto me, that he would give unto me, and unto my seed, the land for an everlasting possession.

8 Therefore, O my son, he hath blessed me in raising thee up to be a servant unto me, in saving my house from death;

9 In delivering my people, thy brethren, from famine which was sore in the land; wherefore the God of thy fathers shall bless thee, and the fruit of thy

loins, that they shall be blessed above thy brethren, and above thy father's house;

10 For thou hast prevailed,[59] and thy father's house hath bowed down unto thee, even as it was shown unto thee, before thou wast sold into Egypt by the hands of thy brethren; wherefore thy brethren shall bow down unto thee, from generation to generation, unto the fruit of thy loins forever;

11 For thou shalt be a light unto my people, to deliver them in the days of their captivity, from bondage; and to bring salvation unto them, when they are altogether bowed down under sin.[60]

Ephraim was born in Egypt before the arrival of the children of Israel from Canaan. The *Book of Numbers* lists three sons of Ephraim: Shuthelah, Beker, and Tahan. However, *1 Chronicles 7* claims that he had at least eight sons, including Ezer and Elead, who were killed by local men who came to rob him of his cattle. After their deaths he had another son, Beriah. He was the ancestor of Joshua, son of Nun, the leader of the Israelite tribes in the conquest of Canaan. When the Tribe of Levi failed at the Golden Calf and at the Spilt Rock of Horeb, the Lord gave the right to lead the family into the promised land to the birthright holders under Joshua, the chief prince of Ephraim. He did not want the kingly tribes to do it (Judah and Benjamin) because the Lord Himself is the only true king of Israel.

According to the biblical narrative, Jeroboam, who became the first king of the Northern Kingdom of Israel, was also from the house of Ephraim.

Manasseh was Joseph's eldest son but he was placed in second place by Father Israel at the time of the transferring of the Birthright Blessing.

Manasseh had two sons, one named Asriel with his wife and one named Machir with an Aramean concubine *(see 1 Chronicles 7:14)*. *Numbers 32:41* and *Deuteronomy 3:14* refer to a son called

Jair, who "took all the region of Argob, as far as the border of the Geshurites and the Maachathites, and [who] called Bashan after his own name, Havoth Jair."

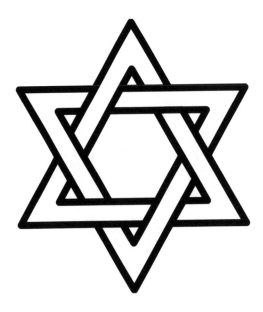

Chapter Fourteen

The Plates of Brass

Are not these things written upon the Plates of Brass of our fathers?
— King Mosiah

The war between Christianity and Judaism (which will someday be called the war between Ephraim & Judah)[61] will be understood more clearly with the restoration of the *Brass Plates* which were, in the last documented possession of the children of Lehi, known as the Nephites.

The purposeful manipulation of history, and sacred text by both the *Church of the Devil* and the *Synagogue of Satan*, to quote the Lord, is not yet clearly understood by the world at large. In terms of Christianity, fault resides primarily with the bishops of Rome and their Edomite agenda to rule in the place of Christ; a design which goes all the way back to Nimrod and Mystery Babylon. In Jewry, the same need stems from the basic loss of the Pharisees and the need of the Sadducees to move prophetic scripture away from Jesus Christ. The problem was this — Jesus really was the promised Messiah, and as such, prophecy and scripture prior to Him testified of Him, openly. This is hard for us to get our minds around today. Let's take a short tangent on the history of the Pharisees and the Sadducees to help explain why modern Christianity and Judaism are in their present state.

A BRIEF HISTORY OF THE PHARISEES & SADDUCEES

Most students of the *Bible* take too many things for granted. We gospel feasters have learned to stop and ask questions in faith and see what juicy tidbits our inquiring minds uncover. This is a righteous act. The Lord has told us to knock and He will answer, to study things out in our minds and He will teach us. By the time most of us reach the *New Testament* and read about the Pharisees and the Sadducees, we say, "Oh, yes those guys who gave Jesus so much trouble. You know the Pharisees and the Sadducees." That's all good, except that we feasters don't do that anymore. We stop and say, "Wait a minute? If the *Old Testament* ends with the Levites and the Prophets, who are these Pharisees and Sadducees and why haven't we heard about them before now?" Great question! It happened like this.

In the beginning all priesthood was the *Priesthood of the Son of God*. It was so holy that men started calling it the *Melchizedek Priesthood* after our Great Father Shem, who ruled as patriarch of Salem, and head of the House of Shem. In terms of birth order he was the second son of Noah, being forty years younger than his brother Japheth. He would become the greatest of Noah's sons. Sadly we know very little about him today and almost none of it is authoritative. We do have some legends and suppositions which we explored together in *Volume 8* of our study in *Genesis*.

Of the descendants of Melchizedek, Abraham would prevail with the Lord and secure the *Abrahamic Covenant*, which if embraced fully on the Lord's terms, guarantees both salvation and exaltation for all. Abraham held the same priesthood authority as both Noah and Shem. It is our restored understanding that it was conferred upon him by Shem; although Jewish legend says it was Noah.[62] This same priesthood continued through Isaac to Jacob and onto the heads of his Twelve Sons, the most righteous of which was Joseph. Abraham also ordained his worthy sons by his wife Keturah. One of these was Jethro. Due to the *Dead Sea Scrolls*, we now understand why Moses had to receive the priesthood via Jethro. His own father, who was righteous and could have done it, was not in Egypt at the time of his birth and was bared from his family for over 40 years. This is part of the reason that his mother Jochebed had to hide him from Pharaoh's guards. She had no adult male support to protect or hide their baby son. Moses grew up an Egyptian and did not receive his education in Semitic righteousness until he was mentored in such by his father-in-law who was a righteous High Priest over the land of Media. This is the same area which would give rise to Islam's Muhammad. Personally I believe that it was Muhammad's desire to be like Jethro (who may have been his ancestor) which led him to pursue religion in the name of Abraham.[63]

It was the Lord's intention to take the children of Israel, (which may have been 3 million strong at that time) out of Egyptian captivity and cut a new covenant with them at Sinai.[64] This new covenant was to be a marriage contract where the pre-mortal Jesus Christ – called in English, Jehovah – would join with Israel in marriage and thereby gift them, all that the Father committed to the Son! This was a sign of atonement in that under the laws of God and man, a husband and his wife are one flesh.

This is what made the debacle of the Golden Calf so egregious to the Lord. He had literally come down from heaven with the most intimate atoning covenant given to date and His betrothed – the one He had promised Abraham to protect – was having an orgy at the foot of the wedding canopy! No, it could not have been worse. The Lord was so mad that had Moses not talked Him down, He would have killed off the entire house of Israel. You can read all about that in *Exodus*.[65] As a less drastic measure, He instead took Moses's brother Aaron and ordained him and his sons to a truncated priesthood which contained all of the necessary powers to prepare for the coming of the Messiah, as well as take care of those good works, which if performed during one's lifetime would be enough to secure greater blessings in the future. It was a terrible slap to the men of Israel most of all. Males, made in the image of God, were fore-ordained to take upon them the masculine power of God, which is the priesthood. Being denied such, and having to go to another male of the clan, is humbling. It was meant to be humbling. The entire purpose of the Mosaic Law was to humble Israel into actually keeping their commitment to prepare a house ready to receive the Messiah. Paul understood this:

Romans 5:20 ...the law [of Moses] entered, that the offence might abound. But where sin abounded, grace did much more abound.

This can be a difficult thing to get our minds around. What it is saying is that the Lord God gave Israel a law they couldn't keep to humble them. Gasp! But, what about the Mormon clause that God gives no command to man except that He prepare a way? Hold that thought, Paul was way ahead of you. Read it again with this helpful translation:

Romans 5:20 The law [of Moses] was given to humble Israel and show them their sinful natures. But where their sin increased, the power of the Lord's grace was made more manifest.

21 Even though their sins caused their spiritual deaths, Christ's grace reigned supreme. His righteousness became their example and means of eternal life.

In other words, Nephi was right. God did provide a way. He took upon Him our sins. The greatest of all, the Anointed One that was Promised, the Son of God, would be man enough to do what we could not. Today we must help prepare the way for His righteousness. He will explain all our concerns when He comes.

We learned from the *Testimony of Levi* that there was a prophecy that the purity of the priesthood given to the Levites would corrupt over time until it because basically worthless. It was the sad ministry of Elijah to temporarily "loose" the

Celestial binding of the betrothal which Moses set in place. The Celestial *binding and loosing* of a marriage is a right of the Melchizedek Priesthood; authority higher than that which the Levite's possessed at that time. Exactly where Elijah got the Melchizedek President is an enigma. Of great interest to Latter-day Saints is an obscure Jewish tradition which says that Elijah was actually Phinehas, the righteous son of Eleazar, who was the son of Aaron. It also says that he was ordained to the Melchizedek priesthood rights before they were lost to Israel. We will explore this possibility more in another feast, but if true, it does answer some otherwise difficult questions in regard to who Elijah was and where he got his priesthood keys.

Over the next 500 years, the priesthood would become increasingly corrupted. Two bright spots worth mentioning were the sons of Zadok in the days of Solomon, and John the Baptist's father Zacharias. We will come back to him.

The famous religious sects of this study – the Pharisees & Sadducees – came into existence in-between the *Old* and *New Testaments*. We have already studied in *Zechariah* how the Lord restored the Levitical Priesthood after the Babylonian captivity, but the Kingdom of Judah was under the thumb of the Medo-Persians and then the Greeks. It was near the end of the Greek administration over Israel, just as Edomite Rome was on the rise, that a civil war broke out in Judea.

The ruling Seleucids, like the Ptolemys before them, held a mild suzerainty over Judea.[66] They respected Jewish culture and protected Jewish institutions until Antiochus IV changed the policy. According to the *Books of the Maccabees*, while Antiochus was busy in Egypt, a rumor spread that he had been killed. In Judea, the deposed High Priest Jason gathered a force of 1,000 soldiers and made a surprise attack on the city of Jerusalem. Menelaus, the false High Priest appointed by Antiochus, was forced to flee Jerusalem during the riot. King Antiochus Epiphanes returned from Egypt in 168 B.C., enraged by his defeat and very much alive, he attacked Jerusalem and restored Menelaus to power, then executed many rebellious Jews. Here's the account from *2 Maccabees:*

2 Maccabees 5:11-14 When these happenings were reported to the king, he thought that Judea was in revolt. Raging like a wild animal, he set out from Egypt and took Jerusalem by storm. He ordered his soldiers to cut down without mercy those whom they met and to slay those who took refuge in their houses. There was a massacre of young and old, a killing of women and children, a slaughter of virgins and infants. In the space of three days, eighty thousand were lost, forty thousand meeting a violent death, and the same number being sold into slavery.

Antiochus decided to side with the Hellenized Jews in order to consolidate his empire and to strengthen his hold over the region. He outlawed Jewish religious rites and traditions kept by observant Jews and ordered the worship of Zeus as the supreme god. This was anathema to the Orthodox Jews and they refused, so Antiochus sent an army to enforce his decree. The city of Jerusalem was destroyed because of the resistance, many were slaughtered, and Antiochus established a military Greek citadel called the Acra. This occurred around 167 B.C.

After Judah Maccabee led the successful revolt against Antiochus Epiphanes two years later, his brother, Simon Maccabaeus, founded the Hasmonean Dynasty. It would encompass the neighboring regions of Samaria, Galilee, Iturea, Perea, and Idumea. Many scholars call this period a time of independence for Judah. It was not long before both the crumbling Greek Empire and the rising Roman Empire both declared the peoples of Israel as independent.[67] Trouble started when John Hyrcanus, following the Pharaonic model declared himself both King and High priest; a combination that was forbidden by Moses. The sect that supported his claim over both church and state called themselves "Sadducees" in honor of Zadok, the High Priest who anointed King Solomon. Zadok is an honorific of Melchizedek who was both High Priest and King; based on his patriarchal right. They believed that they had the right to force everyone in their realm to convert to Judaism. For the males in the region, this meant forced circumcision. Soon a group of objectors rose who called themselves "separatists" in Hebrew. They were the Pharisees. They believed that the priestly code of conduct was required only of the priests, and that the Mosaic Law could not be forced upon non-Jews, even if they lived on Jewish lands.

When Alexander Jannaeus took the throne, he pushed his authority one step further and ordered that all living in Judaean lands were bound by law to follow the code set down by the priests. It was a sort of early Sharia law. This decree brought about the Pharisaic Revolt, an eight year civil war lasting from 96 B.C. to 88 B.C.

When the Pharisees at last got the upper hand, they placed a woman, Queen Salome of Alexandria, on the throne. Her brother, who was also president of the Sanhedrin, ordered that public schools be opened with mandatory attendance. This undermined the long held tradition that a father taught his own sons the law, the language, and culture of Moses. The people saw the move as forced indoctrination. It only got worse when he placed two Assyrian friends, who had converted to Judaism earlier, in the Sanhedrin. These changed the accepted understanding of Moses's Laws into what is today called the *Midrash*. It began the so-called "oral tradition" of the Law. It basically meant that the law would be whatever the Sanhedrin said the law meant. A modern example might be found in our own *Word of Wisdom*. A simple reading of the text mentions avoiding "hot drinks." Ask any Mormon what this means and you will be told "no tea or coffee." Okay, but what about "Hot Chocolate?" "No, that's fine." "Okay, what about Ice Tea, then?" "No that's not okay." "What about Yerba Mate?" *Who knows?* We could go on and on until nobody knows who's on first or what's on second. Anglicized Jews would say, "Until Who is He and He is She." Joseph Smith would just say, "Get the Spirit." When one gets the spirit the answer is, "Being set free through the blood of Jesus Christ, it is a form of mockery to make yourself an addict to the body." The heart of the *Word of Wisdom* is to live free in the freedom granted by the Atonement of Jesus Christ and avoid all addictive substances. It also contains a promise which I can personally testify is true. It's found in *Doctrine & Covenants 89:19*. The source of all our *Gospel Feasts* start with that promise.

The Sanhedrin declared that all their interpretations were binding on the people and would be through all time. This was the world that Jesus Christ was born into. His frustration with the Elders of Israel in His day, and their insistence that He was a rebel and a sinner, stems from this exact point. The Pharisees and Sadducees were now the interpreters of the law and the Sanhedrin had the power to enforce their interpretations.

It was around this time that the Essenes of Qumran came on the scene. They agreed with the Pharisees that forced conversion was evil but they refused to accept the *Midrash* or the dictums of the Sanhedrin as legally binding. They held that the scriptures alone were the standard by which all law was to be judged. They removed themselves from the greater community to live their own lives, their own way, in the desert.

ONE LAST POINT

In the end, the most important difference between the Pharisees & Sadducees would be their belief in the After Life. The Pharisees believed that the scriptures clearly taught a Resurrection. The Sadducees did not. They believed that once you were dead that was it — Nothing. You can remember this important difference with the pithy saying: "Why are the Sadducees sad? Because they don't believe in the Resurrection. That is why they are *sad-you-see.*" After Jesus rose from the dead, it was the Pharisees who understood it, and became in time the first Christians. This left only the Sadducees in Judaism, hence the tragedy today of a Jewish funeral. They believe that once you are dead it is over forever. That is why they are *sad-you-get-it?*

CONCEALED & REVEALED

Secular-christians today are confused in their self-righteous assertion that all that they have today in terms of religious knowledge is all that man ever had. Their ministers have a pithy saying which illustrates the point: "The Old Testament is the New Testament concealed but the New Testament is the Old Testament revealed!" True enough, but it belies their misunderstanding with what actually happened. Joseph Smith to the rescue!

The prophet explained that the complete picture of the Gospel was had in every dispensation. Note his brilliant reasoning as he was explaining a statement made by Paul to the Galatians. This one here:

Galatians 3:7 Know ye therefore that they which are of faith, the same are the children of Abraham.

8 And the scripture, foreseeing that God would justify the heathen through faith, preached before the gospel unto Abraham, saying, In thee shall all nations be blessed.

In attempting to explain this, the Prophet reasoned thusly before the Saints:

It will be noticed that according to Paul, the gospel was preached to Abraham. We would like to be informed in what name the gospel was then preached, whether it was the name of Christ or some other name. If in any name, was it the gospel then? And if it was the gospel, and that preached in the name of Christ, had it any ordinances [meaning works]? If not, was it really the gospel then? And if they did have ordinances, what were they? Our christian friends might say: perhaps they had no ordinances except offering blood sacrifice before the coming of Christ, and that it could not be possible for the gospel to have been administered while the sacrifices of blood were. But we will recollect that Abraham offered sacrifice and notwithstanding this had the gospel preached to him. That the offering of sacrifice was not only to point the mind forward to Christ we infer from these remarkable words of his to the Jews found in John 8:56: "Your father Abraham rejoiced to see my day: and he saw it, and was glad." So, then, because the ancients offered sacrifice it did not hinder their hearing the gospel but served, as we said before, to open their eyes and enable them to look forward to the time of the coming of the Savior, and to rejoice in his redemption.[68]

This means that the saving works, and the very name of Jesus Christ (in one form or another) was known in every age. Thus the *Old Testament* was concealed but only because of wicked and conspiring men. We will yet explain the need for the *Brass Plates*, but let us use an example to prove our point first, the ancient and just studied: *Testimony of the Patriarchs*.

The *Testimony of the Patriarchs* purports to be the dying testimonies of the 12 sons of Israel written in Egypt by the command of both their father Israel and the Lord God. They have always been part of the Jewish cannon and were handed down through the tribes from the very day they were written. These books so openly testify of Jesus Christ that later Jewish scholars were forced to insist that they were Christian forgeries. Since they were Jewish books, Christian scholars upon reading them, believed the Jewish Rabbis who denounced them. Thus, they were regulated to the ash heap of Medieval made up

Christian literature. All of that changed in 1946 A.D., with the discovery of the *Dead Sea Scrolls*. The world had egg on their faces when some of these so-called "fake Medieval Christian made-up books" where found in these ancient, pre-christian scrolls. This means that these books were had in the years prior to Jesus Christ. They therefore stand with *Daniel* and many, many other so-called "apocryphal" works proving Joseph Smith's point.

The Jews of yesteryear flocked to Jesus of Nazareth because they were expecting Him, and at the very time he appeared, because of books like this one. These were the signs of their times that Jesus more than once reminded them off during His earthly ministry. The First Christians were born of the Jews and the Pharisees. When they left Jewry with the records, all that was left were the Edomites, the Sadducees, the Samaritans and the Jews who didn't believe Jesus but more specifically those who didn't want Him. This is the reason our Lord wept in Jerusalem. His rejection was a personal rejection. Those in power knew He was the one chosen to come but they didn't want HIM! HIM, personally. That is what really happened. See for yourself:

Matthew 26: 57 And they that had laid hold on Jesus led him away to Caiaphas the high priest, where the scribes and the elders were assembled...

59 Now the chief priests, and elders, and all the council, sought false witness against Jesus, to put him to death;

60 But found none: yea, though many false witnesses came, yet found they none. At the last came two false witnesses,

61 And said, This fellow said, I am able to destroy the temple of God, and to build it in three days.

Then one of them said, "I heard Jesus say that he could destroy the very Temple of Harold and then rebuild it in three days!"

62 And the high priest arose, and said unto him, Answerest thou nothing? what is it which these witness against thee?

But Jesus said nothing in his defense which angered the High Priest who yelled at him, "You say nothing! What have you to say to this charge?"

63 But Jesus held his peace. And the high priest answered and said unto him, I adjure thee by the living God, that thou tell us whether thou be the Christ, the Son of God.

Still Jesus calmly had nothing to say, so the High Priest tried a different tactic. He said, "I demand of you in the name of the living God that you tell us if you are the Messiah we have been waiting for or not. Are you the promised Son of God?"

64 Jesus saith unto him, Thou hast said: nevertheless I say unto you, Hereafter shall ye see the Son of man sitting on the right hand of power, and coming in the clouds of heaven.

Then Jesus spoke. He answered, "You are the ones who are calling me that, however, I will tell you this much, after today you will next see me sitting in the Messiah's seat and returning to the Earth in the clouds of heaven."

65 Then the high priest rent his clothes, saying, He hath spoken blasphemy; what further need have we of witnesses? behold, now ye have heard his blasphemy.

66 What think ye? They answered and said, He is guilty of death.

"There!" cried the High Priest, "We don't need any more witnesses at all. You heard him blaspheme by his own mouth and now all of you have heard it too! What should we do about this?" And the assembly answered, "Kill him."

These events take on clearer significance now that we understand the holy writ which made up the Jewish experience in Jesus's day. With the return of the *Dead Sea Scrolls* we have at last a more complete answer. The Lord was rejected exactly for the reason Isaiah said He was. Re-read and understand the tragedy:

Isaiah 53:1 Who hath believed our report?...

2 For [the Messiah] shall grow up before [God] as a tender plant, and as a root out of a dry ground: he hath no form nor comeliness; and when we shall see him, there is no beauty that we should desire him.

3 He is despised and rejected of men; a man of sorrows, and acquainted with grief: and we hid as it were our faces from him; he was despised, and we esteemed him not.

The scriptures speak the truth. Our Lord's rejection was a personal one. The people met Him and didn't want HIM. It was personal. That's what makes it so tragic.[69] The *Dead Sea Scrolls* prove it. Let's take a short tangent on the History of the *Dead Sea Scrolls* and then circle back to the *Plates of Brass.*

THE DEAD SEA SCROLLS

We opened this feast with a history of the Pharisees and Sadducees and also met a third group, the independent Essenes who wanted nothing to do with either of them. Today we know that the Essenes kept a library of ancient sacred texts at their settlement called Qumran. We know that prior to the Roman destruction of the Temple, they sealed their library in earthen jars and hid them in caves near the Dead Sea in the hopes of saving them. This occurred prior to 70 A.D., in the early years of the young Christian Church. From that time on, Bedouins would occasionally discover scrolls in desert caves in the area and sell them to interested parties. We still have record of the Orthodox Christian Church of Syria posting an offer in the 11th century to buy any cave scrolls that were found, particularly those of Biblical significance.

During the centuries, various additional books were discovered and made their way into the hands of Christians. One such set of scrolls was the *Testimony of the Patriarchs,* the sons of Israel; the one we are studying now. The Christians reading these books were blown away to discover the candid teachings about the Saviour Jesus Christ, and the fulfillment of prophecy recorded plainly therein. Missionary efforts to the Jews, and others, used these books to say, "See, Jesus was the Messiah as promised." Powerful Rabbis, attempting to curb the momentum, declared these books to be obvious Medieval Christian forgeries. Later with the rise of so-called European Rationalism, Mahanism, and Darwinism, it was said that there was no God. So, any book claiming to be prophetic had to be a forgery written after the events described, since no man can know the future. Thus, the very proof that they were from God was used against them.[70] Man began to doubt these books and set them aside. Protestants were convinced that evil popes had invented them along with the many things they did invent in their grab for power.[71] When the *Dead Sea Scrolls* were found, beginning in 1948 A.D., the doubters had egg on their faces. Here were many of the books that had been declared to be Medieval Christian inventions. They couldn't be. These books were older than Jesus Christ. In fact, He would have had access to many of them. Here is what we understand today, and how it pertains to Lehi's *Plates of Brass.*

The ancient Jews and Rabbis have said that while the *Books of Moses* legally belong to every household in Israel, there was another set of scriptures which contained the *Testimonies of the Nation.* One might compare these to the various plates of Nephi. Nephi had a set of plates that he called *The Large Plates of Nephi* which contained the civil history of the people, their wars, travels and kings. Then he had another set of plates he called *The Small Plates of Nephi.* These contained his testimony, personal journal, important sermons, and spiritual thoughts. It was sort of like a religious history. Israel in the old world worked the same. The *Talmud* tells us that every patriarch and prophet of Israel wrote their life story, testimony and history, particularly their dealings with God in their time as a gift for their children. It was more than a gift, it was considered their sacred duty.[72] It is in keeping with this heavenly command, that the Sons of Israel wrote the books we have just read. They were carrying on a tradition and a commandment from… wait for it… from the days of Adam, himself.

This means that every single righteous father from Adam to Ezra kept a journal and added it to the master set of records, safe guarded for the people. Various copies could be made from the archive but, while not every one wanted or needed every journal, since not all of them were equally prized or needed by every family, the whole was available to any interested reader. From the *Dead Sea Scrolls*, we have fragments, whole chapters, and whole books restored to us which prove this ancient legend is true.

In addition to proving the authenticity of the testimonies of the sons of Israel (and their prophecies about the coming of Jesus of Nazareth) we now have fragments of the original personal records of pre-flood Enos, Enoch, and Lamech. After the flood we have fragments of the books of Noah, Abraham, Jacob, Levi, Levi's son Kohath, Moses's father Amram and Aaron the Priest! What's more, in terms of the *Testimonies of the Patriarchs*, the *Dead Sea Scrolls* fragments and books read the same as the Medieval Christian copies.[73] Of interest in a future feast, many copies of the *Book of Jubilees* were found which claim that it was the sixth book of Moses. Careful study shows that Jesus Christ quoted *Jubilees* as scripture during his early ministry. Indeed some of his more enigmatic sermons and parables only make sense in light of Moses's sixth book. *Jubilees* tells us that all of these records were entrusted to Levi who was to hold them for the nation and guard them forever.

Now we get back to the *Book of Mormon* and the *Plates of Brass*. The Jews say that sometime prior to the fall of Jerusalem, the master set of all these testimonies disappeared. Their loss to the world, and all peoples who hold to Biblical truths and culture, is a colossal disaster! It is now assumed that they were destroyed by Nebuchadnezzar and lost forever, but note the power of the Lord God of Israel. Here is what really happened to that well guarded, master set of priceless testimony:

THE PLATES OF BRASS

1 Nephi 2:1 For behold, it came to pass that the Lord spake unto my father, yea, even in a dream, and said unto him: Blessed art thou Lehi, because of the things which thou hast done; and because thou hast been faithful and declared unto this people the things which I commanded thee, behold, they seek to take away thy life.

2 And it came to pass that the Lord commanded my father, even in a dream, that he should take his family and depart into the wilderness.

3 And it came to pass that he was obedient unto the word of the Lord, wherefore he did as the Lord commanded him.

4 And it came to pass that he departed into the wilderness. And he left his house, and the land of his inheritance, and his gold, and his silver, and his precious things, and took nothing with him, save it were his family, and provisions, and tents, and departed into the wilderness...

How many times in history has a man or woman left all of their precious things behind and ran into the wilderness to protect their families? *Not as many times as you'd think.*

1 Nephi 3:2 And it came to pass that he spake unto me, saying: Behold I have dreamed a dream, in the which the Lord hath commanded me that thou and thy brethren shall return to Jerusalem.

3 For behold, Laban hath the record of the Jews and also a genealogy of my forefathers, and they are engraven upon plates of brass.

4 Wherefore, the Lord hath commanded me that thou and thy brothers should go unto the house of Laban, and seek the records, and bring them down hither into the wilderness.

5 And now, behold thy brothers murmur, saying it is a hard thing which I have required of them; but behold I have not required it of them, but it is a commandment of the Lord.

6 Therefore go, my son, and thou shalt be favored of the Lord, because thou hast not murmured.

7 And it came to pass that I, Nephi, said unto my father: I will go and do the things which the Lord hath commanded, for I know that the Lord giveth no commandments unto the children of men, save he shall prepare a way for them that they may accomplish the thing which he commandeth them.

8 And it came to pass that when my father had heard these words he was exceedingly glad, for he knew that I had been blessed of the Lord.

Why was this such a big deal? It was because this was the master set of scriptures. The one that the Jews say disappeared even though they were well guarded.

9 And I, Nephi, and my brethren took our journey in the wilderness, with our tents, to go up to the land of Jerusalem.

10 And it came to pass that when we had gone up to the land of Jerusalem, I and my brethren did consult one with another.

11 And we cast lots — who of us should go in unto the house of Laban. And it came to pass that the lot fell upon Laman; and Laman went in unto the house of Laban, and he talked with him as he sat in his house.

12 And he desired of Laban the records which were engraven upon the plates of brass, which contained the genealogy of my father.

13 And behold, it came to pass that Laban was angry, and thrust him out from his presence; and he would not that he should have the records. Wherefore, he said unto him: Behold thou art a robber, and I will slay thee.

14 But Laman fled out of his presence, and told the things which Laban had done, unto us. And we began to be exceedingly sorrowful, and my brethren were about to return unto my father in the wilderness.

15 But behold I said unto them that: As the Lord liveth, and as we live, we will not go down unto our father in the wilderness until we have accomplished the thing which the Lord hath commanded us.

16 Wherefore, let us be faithful in keeping the commandments of the Lord; therefore let us go down to the land of our father's inheritance, for behold he

left gold and silver, and all manner of riches. And all this he hath done because of the commandments of the Lord.

17 For he knew that Jerusalem must be destroyed, because of the wickedness of the people.

18 For behold, they have rejected the words of the prophets. Wherefore, if my father should dwell in the land after he hath been commanded to flee out of the land, behold, he would also perish. Wherefore, it must needs be that he flee out of the land.

19 And behold, it is wisdom in God that we should obtain these records, that we may preserve unto our children the language of our fathers;

20 And also that we may preserve unto them the words which have been spoken by the mouth of all the holy prophets, which have been delivered unto them by the Spirit and power of God, since the world began, even down unto this present time.

21 And it came to pass that after this manner of language did I persuade my brethren, that they might be faithful in keeping the commandments of God.

22 And it came to pass that we went down to the land of our inheritance, and we did gather together our gold, and our silver, and our precious things.

23 And after we had gathered these things together, we went up again unto the house of Laban.

24 And it came to pass that we went in unto Laban, and desired him that he would give unto us the records which were engraven upon the plates of brass, for which we would give unto him our gold, and our silver, and all our precious things.

25 And it came to pass that when Laban saw our property, and that it was exceedingly great, he did lust after it, insomuch that he thrust us out, and sent his servants to slay us, that he might obtain our property.

26 And it came to pass that we did flee before the servants of Laban, and we were obliged to leave behind our property, and it fell into the hands of Laban.

27 And it came to pass that we fled into the wilderness, and the servants of Laban did not overtake us, and we hid ourselves in the cavity of a rock.

28 And it came to pass that Laman was angry with me, and also with my father; and also was Lemuel, for he hearkened unto the words of Laman. Wherefore Laman and Lemuel did speak many hard words unto us, their younger brothers, and they did smite us even with a rod.

29 And it came to pass as they smote us with a rod, behold, an angel of the Lord came and stood before them, and he spake unto them, saying: Why do ye smite your younger brother with a rod? Know ye not that the Lord hath chosen him to be a ruler over you, and this because of your iniquities? Behold ye shall go up to Jerusalem again, and the Lord will deliver Laban into your hands.

30 And after the angel had spoken unto us, he departed.

Had the angel not appeared, Nephi would have likely been killed by his brothers.

31 And after the angel had departed, Laman and Lemuel again began to murmur, saying: How is it possible that the Lord will deliver Laban into our hands? Behold, he is a mighty man, and he can command fifty, yea, even he can slay fifty; then why not us?

1 Nephi 4:1 And it came to pass that I spake unto my brethren, saying: Let us go up again unto Jerusalem, and let us be faithful in keeping the commandments of the Lord; for behold he is mightier than all the earth, then why not mightier than Laban and his fifty, yea, or even than his tens of thousands?

2 Therefore let us go up; let us be strong like unto Moses; for he truly spake unto the waters of the Red Sea and they divided hither and thither, and our fathers came through, out of captivity, on dry ground, and the armies of Pharaoh did follow and were drowned in the waters of the Red Sea.

3 Now behold ye know that this is true; and ye also know that an angel hath spoken unto you; wherefore can ye doubt? Let us go up; the Lord is able to deliver us, even as our fathers, and to destroy Laban, even as the Egyptians.

4 Now when I had spoken these words, they were yet wroth, and did still continue to murmur; nevertheless they did follow me up until we came without the walls of Jerusalem.

5 And it was by night; and I caused that they should hide themselves without the walls. And after they had hid themselves, I, Nephi, crept into the city and went forth towards the house of Laban.

6 And I was led by the Spirit, not knowing beforehand the things which I should do.

7 Nevertheless I went forth, and as I came near unto the house of Laban I beheld a man, and he had fallen to the earth before me, for he was drunken with wine.

8 And when I came to him I found that it was Laban.

9 And I beheld his sword, and I drew it forth from the sheath thereof; and the hilt thereof was of pure gold, and the workmanship thereof was exceedingly fine, and I saw that the blade thereof was of the most precious steel.

What comes next, may be the hardest thing that Nephi ever had to do. Note carefully how, even in this later account, one can sense the torment and the need to justify and mollify a moment which he could not both fully embrace nor walk away from.

10 And it came to pass that I was constrained by the Spirit that I should kill Laban; but I said in my heart: Never at any time have I shed the blood of man. And I shrunk and would that I might not slay him.

11 And the Spirit said unto me again: Behold the Lord hath delivered him into thy hands. Yea, and I also knew that he had sought to take away mine own life; yea, and he would not hearken unto the commandments of the Lord; and he also had taken away our property.

12 And it came to pass that the Spirit said unto me again: Slay him, for the Lord hath delivered him into thy hands;

13 Behold the Lord slayeth the wicked to bring forth his righteous purposes. It is better that one man should perish than that a nation should dwindle and perish in unbelief.

Nephi is still debating all of this within. Note that:

14 And now, when I, Nephi, had heard these words, I remembered the words of the Lord which he spake unto me in the wilderness, saying that: Inasmuch as thy seed shall keep my commandments, they shall prosper in the land of promise.

15 Yea, and I also thought that they could not keep the commandments of the Lord according to the law of Moses, save they should have the law.

16 And I also knew that the law was engraven upon the plates of brass.

17 And again, I knew that the Lord had delivered Laban into my hands for this cause — that I might obtain the records according to his commandments.

18 Therefore I did obey the voice of the Spirit, and took Laban by the hair of the head, and I smote off his head with his own sword.

19 And after I had smitten off his head with his own sword, I took the garments of Laban and put them upon mine own body; yea, even every whit; and I did gird on his armor about my loins.

20 And after I had done this, I went forth unto the treasury of Laban. And as I went forth towards the treasury of Laban, behold, I saw the servant of Laban who had the keys of the treasury. And I commanded him in the voice of Laban, that he should go with me into the treasury.

21 And he supposed me to be his master, Laban, for he beheld the garments and also the sword girded about my loins.

22 And he spake unto me concerning the elders of the Jews, he knowing that his master, Laban, had been out by night among them.

23 And I spake unto him as if it had been Laban.

24 And I also spake unto him that I should carry the engravings, which were upon the plates of brass, to my elder brethren, who were without the walls.

25 And I also bade him that he should follow me.

This fits the paradigm perfectly. Again, according to the ancients, the master set of scriptures was guarded but available to the sages and people for instruction and reading when needed. There were copies made for various uses onto skin, leather, or papyrus but the master set was kept on metal plates. Laban, with a servant, was taking them to the "elders of Judah," who – note at this phase in their history – were drunks. Still this was a proper request and Laban was in charge of protecting them.

26 And [Laban's servant], supposing that I spake of the brethren of the church, and that I was truly that Laban whom I had slain, wherefore he did follow me.

27 And he spake unto me many times concerning the elders of the Jews, as I went forth unto my brethren, who were without the walls.

28 And it came to pass that when Laman saw me he was exceedingly frightened, and also Lemuel and Sam. And they fled from before my presence; for they supposed it was Laban, and that he had slain me and had sought to take away their lives also.

29 And it came to pass that I called after them, and they did hear me; wherefore they did cease to flee from my presence.

30 And it came to pass that when the servant of Laban beheld my brethren he began to tremble, and was about to flee from before me and return to the city of Jerusalem.

31 And now I, Nephi, being a man large in stature, and also having received much strength of the Lord, therefore I did seize upon the servant of Laban, and held him, that he should not flee.

32 And it came to pass that I spake with him, that if he would hearken unto my words, as the Lord liveth, and as I live, even so that if he would hearken unto our words, we would spare his life.

33 And I spake unto him, even with an oath, that he need not fear; that he should be a free man like unto us if he would go down in the wilderness with us.

34 And I also spake unto him, saying: Surely the Lord hath commanded us to do this thing; and shall we not be diligent in keeping the commandments of the Lord? Therefore, if thou wilt go down into the wilderness to my father thou shalt have place with us.

35 And it came to pass that Zoram did take courage at the words which I spake. Now Zoram was the name of the servant; and he promised that he would go down into the wilderness unto our father. Yea, and he also made an oath unto us that he would tarry with us from that time forth.

36 Now we were desirous that he should tarry with us for this cause, that the Jews might not know concerning our flight into the wilderness, lest they should pursue us and destroy us.

37 And it came to pass that when Zoram had made an oath unto us, our fears did cease concerning him.

38 And it came to pass that we took the plates of brass and the servant of Laban, and departed into the wilderness, and journeyed unto the tent of our father.

Lehi would rejoice when he read for the first time the master set of testimonies and histories which had been kept under guard by watch commander Laban. It was here that he learned that he was actually from the tribe of Joseph, something that he apparently didn't know. I have no doubt that

Lehi read among other things, the very testimonies that we are studying together.

What was the Lord thinking in giving the Master Set of Scriptures to Lehi? Three-fold. He saved them from Nebuchadnezzar. They became the scriptures of the Nephite Nation (helping them preserve their correct heritage, as long as possible) and he got them into the safe keeping of the children of Ephraim, (the birthright tribe) nestled in the stakes of Zion, on the greater land promised to Adam and Enoch as the New Jerusalem. See for yourself:

MAYOR SIMONSEN & AMOS WRIGHT
RECOUNTED BY JOHN HEINERMAN

Sometime during 1911, an old and prominent pioneer figure by the name of Amos Wright came down from Bennington, Bear Lake County, Idaho with two of his grown sons to the Merrill Lumber Company in Brigham City, Utah where Chris Simonsen [born Nels Christian Simonsen] kept his architect's office. Wright had been the ward bishop of his small farming community just north of Montpelier for a number of years. As a teenager he mastered the Shoshone language, which later proved very useful during several church missions that he served among the Indian nations. By the time he was 21 years old, Wright had served as an Indian translator, a freighter, a Pony Express rider, church missionary, and general adventurer.

Wright and his sons were at the lumber yard for several hours. While they took their time in loading some rough-cut dimensional material into the big wagon they brought with them, Wright and Simonsen engaged in a delightful conversation on a variety of topics. Being keenly interested in knowing more about the early history of Utah, the architect pressed the old bishop into telling him incidents from his own early life.

Amos recounted an episode which must have transpired shortly after he gave up riding as a mail courier for the Pony Express. He accompanied two friends about his own age to their homes in Kanab in the southern part of the state. Here he met the famed buckskin Apostle to the Lamanites Jacob Hamblin, who shared a most intriguing tale with Wright and a few other select men one night at the home of Ira Hatch.

Hamblin opened up the conversation by noting that people sometimes had questioned him on why he did so many things among the Lamanites without first consulting with the Church Authorities in Salt Lake City. His standard reply to them always was that while Church President Brigham Young had called and set him apart as a special Apostle to the Indians, he actually took his regular marching orders from the Three Nephites of *The Book of Mormon* fame.

(These were three of the original twelve Disciples whom Jesus Christ appointed to preside over His Church which He established in the Western Hemisphere, in the northern part of Colombia, shortly after His Resurrection. While nine eventually died of old age, three were given the unique blessing of having their physical bodies undergo special changes which enabled them to continue living for many, many centuries without ever growing old and possessing powers similar to those of resurrected angels. In this form, they could come and go as they pleased throughout the earth [and heavens]. They would also no longer be subject to disease or temptations from the Evil One. These Three Nephites are the most prominent characters in early Mormon folklore of the 19th century.

Joseph Smith was asked to name the 3 out of 12 Disciples listed in *3rd Nephi*. He opened the *Book of Mormon* and said: "They are Jeremiah, Zedekiah, and Kumenonhi."

Hamblin was visited upon one particular occasion by two of these Three Nephites. They invited him to accompany them into the great stretch of wilderness expanse directly south of Kanab. At this point in his narrative ex-mayor Simonsen paused long enough to point out that when Bishop Wright rehearsed the affair to him, he emphasized that Hamblin claimed it only took them less than an hour to make this historic journey. And although Hamblin never actually stated it as such, he left the distinct impression with his listeners that his physical conveyance to the spot which he was taken, was done through some kind of supernatural power.

Hamblin apparently didn't think it was important enough or pertinent to his story, to disclose details about the physical appearances of his two semi-immortal hosts... The only attention given to detail was in regard to the place they visited. While not entirely specific (probably for sworn secrecy reasons), the buckskin apostle alluded to the immediate area of their visit as being somewhere near the southern Utah and northern Arizona border below Kanab a distance and in Indian country.

One of his hosts informed him that (at that time) no human had set foot on the ground which they were then standing for a number of centuries! He then stretched forth his hand in front of a large, natural rock wall facing them and an entry way became promptly apparent.

The three of them went inside, one Nephite leading the way, Hamblin in the middle, and his companion bringing up the rear. The inside seemed to be

The Simonsens. <u>Left</u>: Charlottie Merrill Simonsen. <u>Right</u>: Brigham City Mayor and Architect, Nels Christian "Chris" Simonsen.

rather high, wide, and deep. Hamblin used the word cavern several times to describe what the room resembled to him. Everything about it seemed to have been naturally formed instead of bearing man-made signs of expansion or finishing.

Sunlight from outside was swallowed up by a softer brilliance of illumination from within. But as to the source of the internal lightning, Hamblin was never told. His footsteps were directed towards the back part of one section of a limestone wall, against which were stacked numerous stone boxes of varying descriptions. In each of them, he was told by one of his hosts, were contained metallic plates representing the two great ancient cultures which inhabited the Americas several thousand years ago. Inscribed on them were the many histories, prophecies, wars, and general activities of the Jaredites (who came from the Tower of Babel) and their own people (the Nephites), who came from Jerusalem at the time of King Nebuchadnezzar's invasion and subsequent conquest of that city and adjacent land.

Hamblin remained still and said nothing, undoubtedly quite awestruck with what he saw. His informant said that these records had been gathered together in that particular spot over a period of time by divine means, from former places of secretion in other parts of the Americas (presumably from North, Central and South America). And that the time would come when they would be brought forth by designated servants of the Most High and eventually translated into English through the gift and power of God. These would then become the scriptures for all those living during the Millennium, when Satan would be bound for a thousand years and there would be no more wickedness on earth during that time.

The first of those to be translated would be the Brass Plates. They would give a true account of everything which happened from the very beginning of time down to the time of the prophet Jeremiah. What was contained on them would be a much more complete record than what is presently found in the Old Testament. Many of God's mysteries and workings would then become more abundantly manifested, including many things that happened before the Flood, as well as afterwards.

The entire genealogy and true origins of the Lamanites would also be provided. And with this valuable information, an even greater missionary work would then be done among the remnants of these people scattered over the Americas. Such would become the means of leading the more faithful among them into the Restored Gospel, thereby making them a great and powerful people!

Hamblin was promised that he would be an active participant in these events but not in his present flesh (presumably as a resurrected being). Other things were shown and told to him which he could not divulge. But he closed his thrilling tale in the home of Ira Hatch that particular night before an obviously astonished but very small audience, with his testimony. Bishop Wright told Simonsen that when he heard Hamblin's concluding remarks, it seemed to him as if there were a fire welling up inside of him that could not be contained. Hamblin looked around the room with a steady fix on everyone's eyes and soberly declared that ALL the records from which the Book of Mormon had been compiled were safely hid away and well guarded some good distance from where they all resided. He said he had seen these things with his own eyes and heard this report from two of the Three Nephites themselves. He then bore a powerful testimony of the Book of Mormon itself and admonished everyone in that room to read every word and live by its precepts.

When the old bishop finished, Simonsen said that he felt a peculiar feeling creep over him that he couldn't effectively describe. After that, Amos Wright said no more on the subject and acted as if he didn't want to talk about it anymore. The meaning of it then held greater purpose in the young architect's life than later after he entered into business and politics. But Simonsen still considered the episode something more than just a mere novelty, although he wasn't going to stake his testimony on that alone.

Had Oliver Cowdery been able to stay with us, there is no question in my mind, that he would have been one of the men charged with bringing some of these records to light. His gift was as the gift of Moses and Aaron. He was a mighty writer, and a

170

great wordsmith to the prophet and the church. He would have been the means of much beautiful knowledge given in sacred prose. Here is the Lord's thoughts on the matter:

Doctrine & Covenants 8:1 Oliver Cowdery, verily, verily, I say unto you, that assuredly as the Lord liveth, who is your God and your Redeemer, even so surely shall you receive a knowledge of whatsoever things you shall ask in faith, with an honest heart, believing that you shall receive a knowledge concerning the engravings of old records, which are ancient, which contain those parts of my scripture of which has been spoken by the manifestation of my Spirit.

2 Yea, behold, I will tell you in your mind and in your heart, by the Holy Ghost, which shall come upon you and which shall dwell in your heart.

3 Now, behold, this is the spirit of revelation; behold, this is the spirit by which Moses brought the children of Israel through the Red Sea on dry ground.

4 Therefore this is thy gift; apply unto it, and blessed art thou, for it shall deliver you out of the hands of your enemies, when, if it were not so, they would slay you and bring your soul to destruction.

5 Oh, remember these words, and keep my commandments. Remember, this is your gift.

6 Now this is not all thy gift; for you have another gift, which is the gift of Aaron; behold, it has told you many things;

7 Behold, there is no other power, save the power of God, that can cause this gift of Aaron to be with you.

8 Therefore, doubt not, for it is the gift of God; and you shall hold it in your hands, and do marvelous works; and no power shall be able to take it away out of your hands, for it is the work of God.

9 And, therefore, whatsoever you shall ask me to tell you by that means, that will I grant unto you, and you shall have knowledge concerning it.

10 Remember that without faith you can do nothing; therefore ask in faith. Trifle not with these things; do not ask for that which you ought not.

11 Ask that you may know the mysteries of God, and that you may translate and receive knowledge from all those ancient records which have been hid up, that are sacred; and according to your faith shall it be done unto you.

12 Behold, it is I that have spoken it; and I am the same that spake unto you from the beginning. Amen.

FOOLS RUSH IN

So now we know that Joseph Smith was right. The Gospel and the very name of Jesus Christ was known anciently. The rags of scripture we have left show the ravages of the beasts that have walked among us in the name of the godly. They were really wolves, dragons, and demons dressed up as sheep, popes, bankers, landlords, and politicians. They will never shut up until the Lord God Himself shuts their mouths. Since the cat is now out of the bag and the *Testimony of the Twelve Patriarchs* is now proven to be older than the Middle Ages. Godless scholars have had to make up a new reason to discredit them, and keep you from reading them. Get a load of their new rationalization by one of them who will rename nameless because he is shameless:

The following twelve [testimonies of the Sons of Israel] are biographies written between 107 and 137 B.C. They are a forceful exposition, showing how a Pharisee with a rare gift of writing secured publicity by using the names of the greatest men of ancient times.

When you look beyond the unvarnished–almost brutally frank–passages of the text, you will discern a remarkable attestation of the expectations of the Messiah which existed a hundred years before Christ. And there is another element of rare value in this strange series. As Dr. R. H. Charles says in his scholarly work on the Pseudepigrapha: its ethical teaching "has achieved a real immortality by influencing the thought and diction of the writers of the New Testament, and even those of our Lord. This ethical teaching, which is very much higher and purer than that of the Old Testament, is yet its true spiritual child and helps to bridge the chasm that divides the ethics of the Old and New Testaments."

The instances of the influence of these writings on the New Testament are notable in the Sermon on the Mount which reflects the spirit and even uses phrases from these Testaments. St. Paul appears to have borrowed so freely that it seems as though he must have carried a copy of the Testaments with him on his travels.

Thus, the reader has before him in these pages what is at once striking for its blunt primitive style and valuable as some of the actual source books of the Bible.

How is the Lord to reach men of such a mindset? No matter what He says or does, they will not believe Him. He can't do anything with them and so they can't be saved. They are the sons and daughters of Beliar and we are not going to listen to them anymore. This is our Lord's greatest conundrum and why He says things like this:

Luke 16:13,31 No servant can serve two masters: for either he will hate the one, and love the other; or else he will hold to the one, and despise the other... If they hear not Moses and the prophets, neither will they be persuaded, though one rose from the dead.

They will not believe even if someone rises from the dead because they serve Lucifer. It is the same lament of both Joseph Smith and Moroni. First hear Moroni:

Mormon 8:35 Behold, I speak unto you as if ye were present, and yet ye are not. But behold, Jesus Christ hath shown you unto me, and I know your doing.

36 And I know that ye do walk in the pride of your hearts; and there are none save a few only who do not lift themselves up in the pride of their hearts, unto the wearing of very fine apparel, unto envying, and strifes, and malice, and persecutions, and all manner of iniquities; and your churches, yea, even every one, have become polluted because of the pride of your hearts.

Moroni 10:27 And I exhort you to remember these things; for the time speedily cometh that ye shall know that I lie not, for ye shall see me at the bar of God; and the Lord God will say unto you: Did I not declare my words unto you, which were written by this man, like as one crying from the dead, yea, even as one speaking out of the dust?

28 I declare these things unto the fulfilling of the prophecies. And behold, they shall proceed forth out of the mouth of the everlasting God; and his word shall hiss forth from generation to generation.

29 And God shall show unto you, that that which I have written is true...

34 And now I bid unto all, farewell. I soon go to rest in the paradise of God, until my spirit and body shall again reunite, and I am brought forth triumphant

through the air, to meet you before the pleasing bar of the great Jehovah, the Eternal Judge of both quick and dead. Amen.

Joseph Smith, the last of all:

I have intended my remarks for all, both rich and poor, bond and free, great and small. I have no enmity against any man. I love you all; but I hate some of your deeds. I am your best friend, and if persons miss their mark it is their own fault. If I reprove a man, and he hates me, he is a fool; for I love all men, especially these my brethren and sisters...

I don't blame any one for not believing my history. If I had not experienced what I have, I would not have believed it myself...

When I am called by the trump of the archangel and weighed in the balance, you will all know me then. I add no more. God bless you all.

We humbly thank the Lord for righteous and repentant ancestors from Adam to Noah, Abraham to the sons of Israel to our own grandparents. These, in the days of the world's peril, fought, cried, and rejoiced in covenants they made in behalf of their children. They are our Saviours on Mount Zion. We reap their righteousness.

Will our children reap ours?

Will we continue to push forward the gift they granted us?

I think we will.

Jacob Hamblin b. April 6th 1819 - d. August 31st 1886. Called the special apostle to the Lamanites and friend of the Native Peoples of the Americas.

Detail of Jacob's Vision of the Ladder Up to Heaven by
Jacques Reattu,1792.

The Testimony of Jacob called Israel

"For the Supplanter has prevailed with the Lord."

— *the Angel to Jacob*

Proof that the scriptures, which the Lord is restoring, are connected in their witness comes from the detail and cross-referencing they are showing. For example in the *Book of Jubilees*, called by the Jews the *Sixth Book of Moses* and *The Little Genesis*, is this interesting story, which occurred about the time of Benjamin's birth and Rachel's death:

Jubilees 32:21 And Jacob saw in a vision of the night, and behold an angel descended from heaven with seven tablets in his hands, and he gave them to Jacob, and he read them and knew all that was written therein which would befall him and his sons throughout all the ages.

22 And he showed him all that was written on the tablets, and said unto him: "Do not build this place, and do not make it an eternal sanctuary, and do not dwell here; for this is not the place. Go to the house of Abraham thy father and dwell with Isaac thy father until the day of the death of thy father.

23 For in Egypt thou wilt die in peace, and in this land thou wilt be buried with honour in the sepulchre of thy fathers, with Abraham and Isaac.

24 Fear not, for as thou hast seen and read it, thus will. it all be; and do thou write down everything as thou hast seen and read."

25 And Jacob said: "Lord, how can I remember all that I have read and seen?" And he said unto him: "I will bring all things to thy remembrance."

26 And he went up from him, and he awoke from his sleep, and he remembered everything which he had read and seen, and he wrote down all the words which he had read and seen.

Where are these records? Note these fragments from the *Dead Sea Scrolls.*

The Testimony of Jacob Fragment 1: ...All just and upright men shall survive... no deceit or lustful desires will be found... Now, take the tablets and read everything... and all my troubles and all that was to come to pass to me and my house over the coming 147 years appointed to me. And again, the angel said to me, "Take the tablet from my hands..." So, I took them... and behold there was written on them the very day that I would leave there...

Fragment 2: ...and how the Temple would be and how the priests thereof shall be attired; and... their purification rites; and how they would offer sacrifices upon the altar; and how they would eat their portion of the sacrifices throughout the land... who shall let leave the city and go beneath the walls; and form whence they will... before me a land of 2/4s part...

Fragment 3: ... of the land; and thou shalt partake of the fruit of the land and all that is good there, and thou shalt live... shalt be in madness and error; and go into the crooked paths of... wickedness, until in the end you will be to Him as...

That's all we have until the Lord gives us more, but you can bet they are etched into brass on the plates of the same name, awaiting the day of the Lord's grace, or possibly, as President Benson said, the day we collectively plead for more and prove to the Lord that we are honoring what we have, specifically, *The Book of Mormon.*

Dinah & Job

*Kings will perish, rulers disappear, their pride and lustre will pass like a
shadow across a mirror, but my kingdom will persist forever and ever, for glory
and magnificence are in the chariot of my Father. — Job*
Thou art not yet as Job. — Jehovah to Joseph Smith

Jacob had one daughter in all that coop of roosters. She
was fiercely protected by her brothers who took their eastern
charge seriously to be as the pillars of their father's tent and as
the watchmen on their father's wall. When Shechem raped
Dinah one night in a fit of drunken passion, her brothers Simeon
and Levi murdered every male in the city. Dinah wept much over
her defilement, believing that she could never be happy again.
She believed that no good man would ever want her, but the
Lord had a prince in waiting, one who had also passed through
great sorrows himself.

Most people today don't realize that there is a reason why
Job is included in the *Old Testament.* Job was the son-in-law of
Israel. He married Dinah after the Lord smote his first family.
She was his reward after his tragedy. This was also a blessing to
her since she was in need of an honorable husband.

The Rabbis say that Job was "the most pious Gentile who
ever lived." He was given the title *Servant of God* and his name
would have followed Jacob's in the Lord's moniker *The God of
Abraham, Isaac, Jacob & Job* had he not murmured right at the end
of his trial. Job's full name was Jobab and he was the king of
Edom, also called Uz.[74] Louis Ginzberg made a painstaking
study of Jewish oral and written tradition. We will lean heavily
on his *Life of Job.* It will serve two purposes: one to help us better

understand the world surrounding the patriarchs, and second to flesh out the life of Dinah, the only daughter of Israel:

Job was of double kin to Jacob. He was a grandson of Jacob's brother Esau, and at the same time the son-in-law of Jacob himself, for he had married Dinah as his second wife. He was entirely worthy of being a member of the Patriarch's family, for he was perfectly upright, one that feared God, and eschewed evil.

Tradition has many nice things to say about Job and how he treated his fellow man. As one of the princes of Esau, Job used his wealth and position much as Abraham did, to bless others. It is said that because of this, God blessed him with a mini-taste of what life would be like during the Millennium. Job lived a life of joy and peace.

[Job's] harvests followed close upon the ploughing of his field; no sooner were the seeds strewn in the furrows, than they sprouted and grew and ripened produce. He was equally successful with his cattle.

The Jews like to say that his sheep were able to kill wolves that tried to enter into his flocks and in everything the Lord was with him.

Of sheep he had no less than one hundred and thirty thousand, and he required eight hundred dogs to keep guard over them, not to mention the two hundred dogs needed to secure the safety of his house. Besides, his herds consisted of three hundred and forty thousand asses and thirty-five hundred pairs of oxen. All these possessions were not used for self-indulgent pleasures, but for the good of the poor and the needy, whom he clothed, and fed, and provided with all things necessary. To do all this, he even had to employ ships that carried supplies to all the cities and the dwelling-places of the destitute.

His house was furnished with doors on all its four sides, that the poor and the wayfarer might enter, no matter from what direction they approached. At all times there were thirty tables laden with viands ready in his house, and twelve besides for widows only, so that all who came found what they desired. Job's consideration for the poor was so delicate that he kept servants to wait upon them constantly.

It is said that his guests were so overcome by his example that many would ask to stay and be of service to others. Job would often agree but insisted they accept a fair wage for their services in his house.

If he was asked for a loan of money, to be used for business purposes, and the borrower promised to give a part of his profits to the poor, he would demand no security beyond a mere signature. And if it happened that by some mischance or other the debtor was not able to discharge his obligation, Job would return the note to him, or tear it into bits in his presence.

Job would use his house and wealth as a means of preaching the gospel. After dinner he would lead the feasters in hymns of praise to Jehovah and would rejoice in teaching everyone that the source of his happiness and theirs was the Lord his God.

Most particularly Job concerned himself about the weal and woe of widows and orphans. He was wont to pay visits to the sick, both rich and poor, and when it was necessary, he would bring a physician along with him. If the case turned out to be hopeless, he would sustain the stricken family with advice and consolation. When the wife of the incurably sick man began to grieve and weep, he would encourage her with such words as these: "Trust always in the grace and lovingkindness of God. He hath not abandoned thee until now, and He will not forsake thee henceforth. Thy husband will be restored to health, and will be able to provide for his family as heretofore. But if – which may God forefend – thy husband should die, I call Heaven to witness that I shall provide sustenance for thee and thy children." Having spoken thus, he would send for a notary, and have him draw up a document, which he signed in the presence of witnesses, binding himself to care for the family, should it be bereaved of its head. Thus he earned for himself the blessing of the sick man and the gratitude of the sorrowing wife.

Job tried to teach all of these things to his own children by word and example. When he made offerings unto the Lord as required by Father's Noah and Abraham, he would also make an offering for his children, just in case they had forgotten to do it.

The one trial that Job was not prepared for was destitution. He was a good man but would he be a good man when he was not in-charge, was not rich, was not quickly blessed?

Job was asked once what he considered the severest affliction that could strike him, and he replied, "My enemies' joy in my misfortune, and when God demanded to know of him, after the accusations made by Satan, what he preferred, poverty or physical suffering, he chose pain, saying, "O Lord of the whole world, chastise my body with suffering of all kinds, only preserve me from poverty." Poverty seemed the greater scourge, because before his trials he had occupied a brilliant position on account of his vast wealth.

It was into this setting that Lucifer made his famous charge to the Lord, namely that Job only honored Him because God provide for him abundantly. Satan insisted that the moment Job was disenfranchised, he would curse God and die. The Lord took the challenge. The evil one was told that he could tempt, try, test and destitute Job but was not permitted to take his life. Within a short amount of time, Job lost everything. The lengthy *Book of Job* continues recounting the many friends, sophisticates, and possibly even a few sophists who all came to Job to try and help him make sense of the seemingly senseless. Why would a man so good and so highly favored be brought so low? It was the question that was on everyone's mind.

The book explains (and may be the only one that does) how the Lord is our true advocate and how Lucifer, in the guise of Satan, is our accuser. For some reason, which is not completely apparent in our understanding, a man or woman cannot enter the Celestial worlds if he has any accurate accusers. Much of Lucifer's work is compiling and organizing lists of our sins so that he can throw them in our Father's face at the day of Judgement. We are grateful because our same Father is able to show record in the Book of Life those who have been covered by the blood of the Lamb – His perfect Son, Jesus the Christ.

Job will effectively endure all that Lucifer does to him and will only sin after the loss of his wife, when the peer-pressure of his friends and the world became too great. It is fascinating to notice that after Job's difficult trials the Lord came to him just at the moment of weakness. It is clear from the text that had the Lord delayed another instant, Job would have fallen. As sad as it is to note that Job did not endure in perfection to the end, the Lord was quick to rush to him in his hour of greatest need. This is proof to my heart that the Lord is truly the perfect judge. In His timely rebuke, He corrected Job for his failings but also saved him from greater sin just when he was reaching the crossroads of no return. Ginzberg explains:

The Lord remonstrated with [Job] for his lack of patience, saying: "Why didst thou murmur when suffering came upon thee? Dost thou think thyself of greater worth than Adam, the creation of the own hands, upon whom together with his descendants I decree on account of a single transgression? And yet Adam murmured not. Thou art surely not more worthy than Abraham, whom I tried with many trials, and when he asked, 'Whereby shall I know that I shall inherit the land?' and I replied, 'Know of a surety that thy seed will be a stranger in a land that is not theirs, and shall serve them; and they shall afflict them four hundred years,' he yet murmured not. Thou dost not esteem thyself more worthy than Moses, dost thou? Him I would not grant the favor of entering the promised land, because he spake the words, 'Hear now, ye rebels; shall we bring you forth water out of this rock?' And yet he murmured not. Art thou more worthy than Aaron, unto whom I showed greater honor than unto any created being, for I sent the angels themselves out of the Holy of Holies when he entered the place? Yet when his two sons died, he murmured not."

Ginzberg explains that the contrast between Job and his grandfathers can be illustrated between these two statements: While addressing God's sense of justice in His coming punishment of Sodom & Gomorrah, Abraham said, "Far be it from Thee to slay the righteous with the wicked, that so the righteous should be as the wicked." In other words, "I can't believe Lord that you would ever punish the righteous when you are destroying the wicked." In contrast, Job said, "It is all one;

therefore I say, He destroyeth the perfect and the wicked." Or, "It's all the same. When God is mad, every one suffers the good with the evil." This is a difficult position we put the Lord in. We want to believe that if we are righteous our days will be filled with bliss and sunshine. We expect the Lord to bless the righteous immediately and punish the wicked the second they walk into a casino. This attitude is frequently held in evangelical circles and is totally childish. The Lord does not stand above us with a great hammer smiling down on us the moment we do good and whacking us on the head when we do evil. While He does bless the righteous when they do good, often with the sweet pouring of the Spirit whispering peace; and He does withdraw the Holy Ghost to help us reflect upon sin, this is not the same as instant reward and punishment. Job, like many of us, forgot in the day of our telestial education that life is a journey and a learning experience. We were not sent here to make no mistakes and reap eternal sunshine. Men are that they *might* have joy. When? In the Celestial worlds, in the resurrection, in the arms of family and friends having conquered. Yes, there are moments of joys now but I would argue that these are more moments of peace and spiritual comfort. Study the revelations for yourself and you will see that real joy comes at the judgement day knowing that you have overcome Satan (and yourself) by following in the path of Jesus Christ. It is always expressed in the future, conditional tense. Men are that they might have joy.

Convinced that his suffering was undeserved and unjust, Job had the audacity to say to God: "O Lord of the world, Thou didst create the ox with cloven feet and the ass with unparted hoof, Thou hast created Paradise and hell, Thou createst the righteous and also the wicked. There is none to hinder, Thou canst do as seemeth good in Thy sight."

Job had been a just and good man. When disaster and trial fell upon him, his only answer was "The Lord gives and the Lord takes aways as He wishes." He did not add to that "Blessed Be the Name of the Lord." Job's friends tried to counter by saying, "It's true that God created even the natural man, but he also gave man the scriptures as the remedy so mankind cannot roll their guilt onto God's shoulders and say, 'It's not my fault that God made me this way.'"

The reason Job did not shrink from such extravagant utterances was because he denied the resurrection of the dead. He judged of the prosperity of the wicked and the woes of the pious only by their earthly fortunes. Proceeding from this false premise, he held it to be possible that the punishment falling to his share was not at all intended for him. God had slipped into an error, He imposed the suffering upon him that had been appointed unto a sinner.

This is the reason that God explains His deep knowledge of creation to Job. It is an attempt to say that God knows what is going on in a deeply personal way. It is the height of arrogance for humanity to say that God is out of touch with the conditions and sufferings of earth. God is a highly personal creator with an eye on the individual as well as on the global needs of life. A clear example comes when we see that despite Job's disappointing attitude in his trials, God is also displeased with his friends for passing too harsh a judgement on Job's condition. Job receives mercy because his words and actions are done in the anguish of soul. His friends receive a higher condemnation for their unfair assessment of the situation even though some of their pronouncements are accurate.

Ginzberg would explain that Satan hated Job for his kindness and happy leadership:

The happy, God-pleasing life led by Job for many years excited the hatred of Satan, who had an old grudge against him. Near Job's house there was an idol worshipped by the people. Suddenly doubts assailed the heart of Job, and he asked himself: "Is this idol really the creator of heaven and earth? How can I find out the truth about it?" In the following night he perceived a voice calling: "Jobab! Jobab! Arise, and I will tell thee who he is whom thou desirest to know. This one to whom the people offer sacrifices is not God, he is the handiwork of the tempter, wherewith he deceives men." When he heard the voice, Job threw himself on the ground, and said: "O Lord, if this idol is the handiwork of the tempter, then grant that I may destroy it. None can hinder me, for I am the king of this land."

The Rabbis say that Job was warned by an angel that Satan would mark him for destruction if he attacked idolatry in his kingdom. Job, in his righteous strength called to heaven and said, "Out of love of God I am ready to endure all things unto the day of my death. I will shrink back from nothing." It is said that he then took 50 strong men to the center of false worship and destroyed the idol. I tend to believe this story since it is in keeping with the God that we worship. We have many stories of God forewarning His children of trials in an event to strengthen them. Joseph Smith explained that God does not view our tests and trials on Earth as a game. Secular-christianity teaches that the Lord and Satan are locked in a powerful game of wits and that we are the pawns. Joseph Smith said this was not so. The Lord knowing that Job would suffer beyond the norm if he declared war on Satan, forewarned him. Sure enough, after Job destroyed Lucifer's religion in his kingdom, the evil one sought revenge.

Now Satan betook himself to God, and [asked] Him to put Job into his power, saying: "I went to and fro in the earth, and walked up and down in it, and I saw no man as pious as Abraham. Thou didst promise him the whole land of Palestine, and yet he [still purchased a piece of the land you gave him] as a burial-place for Sarah. As for Job, it is true, I found none that loveth Thee as he does, but if Thou wilt put him into my hand, I shall succeed in turning his heart away from Thee." But God spake, "Satan, Satan, what hast thou a mind to do with my servant Job, like whom there is none in the earth?" Satan persisted in his request touching Job, and God granted it, He gave him full power over Job's possessions [but not his life].

Equipped with unlimited power over the man, Satan plotted to completely destroy him. The Rabbis say that this was done primarily through bringing contention against him by stirring up the hearts of his neighbor's. They say he was attacked on all sides. The Sabaean warriors to the south of him stole his great herds of oxen and donkeys after murdering the men hired to tend them. Job only learned of the disaster when one herdsman escaped the slaughter and told him. The Babylonians, a related house, stole his great flock of sheep.

Satan [next] disguised himself as the king of Persia, [and went among] the city of Job's residence... and spoke to the inhabitants, saying: "This man Job hath appropriated all the goods in the world, leaving naught for others, and he hath also torn down the temple of our god, and now I will pay him back for his wicked deeds. Come with me and let us pillage his house."

It was in the fall of Job's house that all his children were killed. Having borne all of these tragedies well, Satan next turned his evil attack upon Job's physical person.

Satan now caused a terrific storm to burst over the house of Job. He was cast from his throne by the reverberations, and he lay upon the floor for three hours. Then Satan smote his body with leprosy from the sole of his foot unto his crown. This plague forced Job to leave the city, and sit down outside upon an ash-heap, for his lower limbs were covered with oozing boils, and the issue flowed out upon the ashes. The upper part of his body was encrusted with dry boils, and to ease the itching they caused him, he used his nails, until they dropped off together with his fingertips, and he took him a potsherd to scrape himself withal. His body swarmed with vermin...

It is here that the Rabbis say Job's wife told him to pray for death. Job refused. His poor wife held up the best she could. Completely ruined, she hired herself out as a water carrier to other houses, and she had once been a queen. When her new master learned that she was sharing bread with Job the Leper she was fired from this job too. She then cut off her beautiful hair and sold it to buy food for Job.

Satan found her along the way and in disguise said that none of these disasters would have happened if she had not deserved them. It broke her heart and it was in this attitude that she told Job to simply "curse God and die."

It was next that Job would be tested in the one thing he had said he feared most, the eyes of his friends.

The four friends listed in the Book of Job were all part of the family of Esau and were therefore also Job's family. Eliphaz was the king of Teman and was Esau's eldest son. The same who robbed Jacob on the road to Haran years before. Bildad, Zophar and Elihu were three grandsons of Buz who was Job's brother. Buz being a nephew of Abraham.[75]

When the four friends arrived in the city in which Job lived, the inhabitants took them outside the gates, and pointing to a figure reclining upon an ash-heap at some distance off, they said, "Yonder is Job." At first the friends would not give them credence, and they decided to look more closely at the man, to make sure of his identity.

It is said that as they approached him the smell was overpowering. It must have been devastating for Job. The majority of the *Book of Job* deals with the arguments and rationales of Job's friends as they try to make sense of his suffering. It is an important book for the questions it raises, the intelligent arguments and counter arguments it poses as well as the irony in forces upon the reader. We alone have the unique perspective of knowing that Job really did not deserve the trials that came upon him. Of the many discussions in the book, we Gospel Feasters must stop to notice that Bildad questions Job as to the movements of the planets. The Watcher Cult and its connection to Mahanism, Edom and Job's destruction of the idols in his domain, fit perfectly with the broader history we have been exploring. Bildad's questions seem angled toward discovering if Job's mind had been affected as well as his body. Job does his best to answer everyone's questions intelligently and they become convinced that his mind is still intact. He basically reasons that if man cannot understand the movement of matter and food within his own body and how that affects life, how could he possibly understand the movements of the planets and what that means. Further we get insight into how the various famines have affected the greater family of man. Job mentions that he has become as low as the cavemen who live in the outskirts of human society and behave more like animals than men. An eye witness account for sure of the phenomenon of early man which Darwinists and progressives teach our children dates back to pre-dawn. Not so.

His friends will then beg Job to see one of their physicians, but he refuses claiming that God is able to heal him. He still doesn't realize that it is Satan who caused his misfortunate. He argument is simple, "the Lord giveth and the Lord taketh away." Ginzberg adds this:

While the three kings were conversing thus with Job, his wife Zitidos made her appearance clad in rags, and she threw herself at the feet of her husband's friends, and amid tears she spoke, saying: "O Eliphaz, and ye other friends of Job, remember what I was in other days, and how I am now changed, coming before you in rags and tatters."

The sight of the unhappy woman touched them so deeply that they could only weep, and not a word could they force out of their mouths. Eliphaz, however, took his royal mantle of purple, and laid it about the shoulders of the poor woman. Zitidos asked only one favor, that the three kings should order their soldiers to clear away the ruins of the building under which her children lay entombed, that she might give their remains decent burial. The command was issued to the soldiers accordingly, but Job said, "Do not put yourselves to trouble for naught. My children will not be found, for they are safely bestowed with their Lord and Creator."

These words did give some comfort to his wife however. She returned to her employers house and laid down in the cattle barn where she had a bed and died. They say from overwork and exhaustion.

More and more the friends of Job came to the conclusion that he had incurred Divine punishment on account of his sins, and as he asseverated his innocence again and again, they prepared angrily to leave him to his fate. Especially

Elihu was animated by Satan to speak scurrilous words against Job, upbraiding him for his unshakable confidence in God. Then the Lord appeared to them, first unto Job, and revealed to him that Elihu was in the wrong, and his words were inspired by Satan. Next he appeared unto Eliphaz, and to him He spoke thus: "Thou and thy friends Bildad and Zophar have committed a sin, for ye did not speak the truth concerning my servant Job. Rise up and let him bring a sin offering for you. Only for his sake do I refrain from destroying you."

The sacrifice offered by Job in behalf of his friends was accepted graciously by God, and Eliphaz broke out into a hymn of thanksgiving to the Lord for having pardoned the transgression of himself and his two friends. At the same time he announced the damnation of Elihu, the instrument of Satan.

It seems Eliphaz had grown up since his days of being the spoiled brat, lazy, eldest grandson of Isaac and Rebekah.

God appeared to Job once more, and gave him a girdle composed of three ribands, and he bade him tie it around his waist. Hardly had he put it on when all his pain disappeared, his very recollection of it vanished, and, more than this, God made him to see all that ever was and all that shall ever be.

After suffering sevenfold pain for seven years Job was restored to strength. With his three friends he returned to the city, and the inhabitants made a festival in his honor and unto the glory of God. All his former friends joined him again, and he resumed his old occupation, the care of the poor, for which he obtained the means from the people around. He said to them, "Give me, each one of you, a sheep for the clothing of the poor, and four silver or gold drachmas for their other needs."

The trial being past, he was soon restored. Father Jacob gave him his only daughter Dinah; a great gift to her as well, since the ordeal with Shechem had left her believing that she could never have an honorable marriage. She bore Job 10 children; seven sons and three daughters.

When Job, after a long and happy life, felt his end approaching, he gathered his ten children around him, and told them the tale of his days. Having finished the narrative, he admonished them in these words: "See, I am about to die, and you will stand in my place. Forsake not the Lord, be generous toward the poor, treat the feeble with consideration, and do not marry with the women of the Gentiles."

Thereupon he divided his possessions among his sons, and to his daughters he gave what is more precious than all earthly goods, to each of them one riband of the celestial girdle he had received from God.

A sash tied about the middle in eastern thinking is a sign of one's Celestial Mother. It is the umbilical of life that makes one a child of the Father since one's family (and connection to the Father) comes about via His wife. It is said that each of God's human children still retains a "golden umbilical of light" by which our prayers travel all the way back to the womb that is our heavenly home.

For three days Job lay upon his bed, sick though not suffering, for the celestial girdle made him proof against pain. On the fourth day he saw the angels descend to fetch his soul. He arose from his bed, handed a cithern to his oldest daughter Jemimah, "Day," a censer to the second one, Keziah, "Perfume," and a cymbal to the third, Amaltheas, "Horn," and bade them welcome the angels with the sound of music. They played and sang and praised the Lord in the holy tongue. Then he appeared that sits in the great chariot, kissed Job, and rode away bearing his soul with him eastward. None saw them depart except the three daughters of Job.

In true eastern thinking, the names of Job, his wife, most of his children, and his three friends were written in the heavenly *Book of Life*; blessing them forever in remembrance there and here on earth. "Speak the name of the dead," they say, "and the person lives forever!"

As the name of Job will remain imperishable unto all time, by reason of the man's piety, so his three friends were recompensed by God for their sympathy with him in his distress. Their names were preserved, the punishment of hell was remitted unto them, and, best of all, God poured out the holy spirit over them.

Satan had lost, yet again.

About this Series

Continue your feast at **www.GospelFeastBooks.com.**

Volume 1: Daniel & The Last Days

Volume 2: Jonah and the Great Plan of Happiness

Volume 3: Ruth & the Saviours on Mount Zion

Volume 4: Zechariah & the Teachers of Righteousness

Volume 5: Ezekiel & the Millennial Reign of Christ

Volume 6: Revelation & the Mark of the Beast

Volume 7: Genesis & the Sons of the Morning (part 1)

Volume 8: Genesis & the Everlasting Covenant (part 2)

Volume 9 Genesis & the House Divided (part 3)

Volume 10 Genesis & the Messiah Ben Joseph (part 4)

Volume 11 will be on Exodus

Supplemental Vol. A: Ezra & the Great Assembly

Supplemental Vol. B: Gad the Seer & the Corruption of the Covenant

This is Supplemental Vol. C: The Testimonies of the Sons of Israel

Additional Books by the Author:

Tell Me the Story of Joseph (a young person's reader on the life of Joseph Smith the Prophet)

If you would like to be notified when future volumes are available, send an email to Randallco@mac.com and let us know. Don't worry we'll keep your contact information private.

Notes

[1] *see Reuben 2:39.* The problem of being "clean" for Jacob was two-fold, yes there was a spiritual defilement but there was also the concern, at least for the next 9 months anyway, that any child born might have been Reuben's. Her womb therefore was "not pure." It was a woman's chief duty in a family to verify the father of her child. Jacob's only safe answer was to cut off all sexual relations with her; which is not something either of them wanted to do.

[2] This is not 100% accurate. Satan does speak to the mind but his voice is always devious and small-minded. The Lord's voice is pure intelligence, ennobling, and encouraging one to try again, repent, and follow the commandments.

[3] This is brilliant and shows the depth of Reuben's mind and the self reflection he experienced during his days of repentance. It also illuminates with surprising exactness the chief operating secret behind Mahanism, the Watchers, pagan mythology and our modern Alien Abduction experiences (which we will yet discover are all the same thing.)

[4] Reuben was his mother's comfort many times when she felt the isolation of her difficult marriage. Mothers have turned their sons against their fathers and sadly have seen in them the confidant that their husband's are supposed to be. Righteous husbands and wives are to be one, even standing against their own children if need be. We will see this very problem in Judah's family when he gives his testimony to us. Children in the end are better off when their parents function as a unit.

[5] We all know that if a man doesn't check himself, he can work himself up into such a state that his conscience is ignored and the still, small voice goes unheard. The female kingdom struggles with moments of "heat" when desire and emotion is difficult to control. Males have the same problem but their's is more triggered than calendar based. Reuben is saying that he wished he had been more like Joseph and knew to "run away" while the ability to think clearly as a man is still possible.

[6] This is one of the many reasons that I believe these testimonies are accurate. It is fascinating to see how stories alter depending on the teller. As a professional writer, I can say that it is really interesting to see what is said and what is not said in these personal accounts. This is saying that in order to protect Bilhah, Jacob is pretending that an angel told him and not her.

[7] Ultimately the Gods place their love in the correct place. Luciferians believe that the way you "create Legion" within a person is through random and repeated sexual encounters. The idea is that you leave or take within you a piece of every person you have sex with. So in a very real sense it is like idol worship. Place false power and love forever in the wrong place.

⁸ Beliar is one of the old time names of Satan in English. It is a play on the Hebrew Belial, which means "he who gives worthless counsel." Worthless council is as good as a lie, so in English the name was changed to Beliar. Be-liar means "he who embodies lies." He is opposite to God's Be-loved Son who is the embodiment of the Love of our God. Since Lucifer was at this time teaching the crap about him being the good guy misunderstood and that it was the serpent or Lilith or one of the Watchers who was the real villain, his doctrine and teachers were known as those that came from the great liar; the father of all lies, the Beliar.

⁹ Our father Joseph will back all of this up and more in this testimony. It must have been hard on Reuben to reflect on what Joseph was put through and how valiantly he fought to maintain his chastity and how quickly Reuben gave in and hurt the ones he loved.

¹⁰ I am sure that this is in reference to Judah's experiences.

¹¹ I wish that we could completely dismiss the Story of the Watchers but we cannot. Something strange happened pre-flood that gave rise to this reoccurring tale. Both Joseph Smith and Josephus said it was basically a lie. Putting both facts together leaves the conclusion which I believe about it; that it was the beginning of the Mahanistic paradigm on which Lucifer built his own cannon of scripture. The so-called Watcher myth pre-flood is the so-called Alien myth post-flood. It amounts to the systematic controlled breeding of humans (one in the know and one the victim). By drugging the victim, and keeping the perpetrator in-disguise, it is impossible to effectively finger the abusers. If the victims remember anything, they believe that an angel or an alien did the raping. This doesn't fly well with law enforcement. *See Genesis part 1 Vol. 7 for more on this.*

¹² This is the only place where Dan appears in terms of ruling in Israel. Unless this is an error in the text, it may add weight to Joseph Smith's teaching that American's Constitutional Balance of Powers was inspired of God. We do know that in the Millennial governance of earth, Judah will hold the executive powers, Levi will hold the bishopric-priestly powers, and Joseph has the birthright. The word Dan in Hebrew means Judge. Is Reuben saying that Dan's tribe will be as the Judicial branch or government? It is unclear but if true, it is interesting.

¹³ Obviously we are not talking about egregious sins here such as murder, adultery, incest, abuse, etc., so don't miss the point.

¹⁴ Each of the tribes was given a totem sign as a symbol. Reuben's was the only one that was human. His sign was the man. As such, his was the image of the gods, and the very son of God.

¹⁵ This would be the war that eventually lost Israel its freedom.

¹⁶ The greatest of which was Nimrod's Tower of Babel. Edom has always had a fascination with towers and the powerful of the world still do.

¹⁷ The more I study these things, the more I am beginning to believe that the boarders of Egypt reached up higher into what we today call the Holy Land than what is currently understood. If true, it answers some very interesting questions.

¹⁸ This is the only place I know of in scripture that explains the veil of the temple being rent in twain. It is here saying that that was done to show the nakedness of Israel. They had killed their groom and so their own shame (in Celestial terms) their nakedness was shown to all. This adds a fascinating twist to our modern temples, and merely furthers Joseph Smith's teachings. It is just one of so many evidences of Joseph Smith's prophetic calling. He holds up and shows up in so many unexpected places.

¹⁹ The prophecy was that the Lamb of God would be a lamb without spot. When Noah placed a curse on Canaan, it was the same as putting a blemish on him. Modern readers mistake Noah's curse as being on Ham but a careful reading shows that it was on Canaan. It is clear from the text that we do not have the full story here. Either way, when Canaan took the land that Noah had given to Shem, it sparked the problems that would lead all the way up to Armageddon.

²⁰ In Eastern Thinking temples are mountains. That is why the Jews would always say, "Let us go up to Jerusalem" even if they were approaching it from a higher elevation geographically. There is nothing higher on Earth than the temples of the Lord.

²¹ It illustrates an ancient doctrine that while sex may be sex, when a couple conceives, the Lord is there too.

²² I suspect it also had to do with forsaking her father's idols and false gods.

²³ It is comments like this that illustrate the veracity of the testimony. At this exact time humanity was deeply upset with the Lord for shortening the span of human life. Men like Shem were still alive and with lifespans of 600 years compared to Israel's 175, and Joseph's 110 it was obvious that something divine was going on. Issachar is saying in humility, "It's okay if the Lord wills it. Enjoy the time you have been given."

²⁴ Job was a family name. See Appendix B.

²⁵ Interesting list: Dan was the 1st son of Bilhah, Gad was the 1st son of Zilpah, and arguably Simeon was the leading first son after Reuben lost his courage before his father and brethren after dishonoring Bilhah in that night of passion.

²⁶ Daniel would see this very angel. Traditionally it is said that in regards to war, it is Michael and in regards to priestly duties it is Gabriel. See Daniel 9 & 10.

[27] In order to stop this continual sinning before the Lord, the Ten Tribes captured by Assyria, chose not to return to Israel but instead to be led to a new land. The Lord took them northward through Japheth, where along the way, Ephraim fell out and inter-married with the houses of Japheth, turning them into Israel as prophesied by Father Noah in *Genesis 9:27*. Names of locations such as Danube and Dan's Mark are named after Dan while names like Norman, Norse, and Norway all harken back to the Israeli Northmen who journeyed northward through Europe.

[28] With the commission of John the Baptist and then the Lord Jesus Christ, war was made with Satan's kingdom. See *Revelation 12* and *Gospel Feast Vol. 6: Revelation & the Mark of the Beast* for more.

[29] Very interesting. See *Hosea 5:15* for confirmation of this idea.

[30] See *Vol. 5: Ezekiel & the Millennial Reign of Christ*.

[31] see the Personal Writings of Joseph Smith, pg. 481 from a Letter by the Prophet at Nauvoo to members of the 12 in Britain, written December 15th 1840.

[32] The *Book of Abraham* restored to us via Joseph Smith addresses this same concept in a most brilliant way. See *Abraham 3:15-19*.

[33] Both the Lord and Paul would make sermons on this vein. We now know that these books existed in their day and they would have had access to them.

[34] The Hebrews knew that the Earth was a globe and that the planets moved like a great clock on a path in the heavens. It was the pagans and later the Catholic Church that insisted that the world was flat not the Hebrews of the *Bible*.

[35] See *Gad the Seer & the Corruption of the Covenant* supplemental to the Gospel Feast Series for more information.

[36] Joseph was also the only brother, who like his father Israel, prevailed with the Lord. He was able to seize certain blessing for himself and his posterity. *see Genesis 32:22-31*. Joseph's posterity claimed the name Israel ever after, and not even King Solomon's heir Rehoboam contested that when the kingdom was divided. David's house took the name Judah.

[37] see the *Gospel Feast Series* volumes on *Genesis* for more.

[38] *see Isaiah 27:1*. Isaiah knew these books too. They were read in his day.

[39] See the Gospel Feast Series Vol. 2: *Jonah and the Great Plan of Happiness*.

[40] Note the 2 remaining tribes. When the 10 were lost, Judah (representing Leah) and Benjamin (representing Rachel) stayed behind. Both held the kingly lines, Benjamin: Saul, and Judah: David and Jesus Christ.

[41] Rabbi Michael Leo Samuel has this to say: Genesis 41:45 וַיִּקְרָא פַרְעֹה שֵׁם־יוֹסֵף צָפְנַת פַּעְנֵחַ — Pharaoh then gave Joseph the name *Zaphenath-paneah* — Like other foreigners, Joseph assumes an Egyptian name so that he would better fit in Pharaoh's court and be better accepted by the Egyptian people. The meaning of this Egyptian name remains unclear and the certainty of its meaning has eluded scholars since the time of the Septuagint and rabbinic tradition. For example, some early exegetes think the name means, "revealer of secrets." More correctly, R. David Kimchi and Ibn Ezra (ca. 13th century) observe that Zaphenath-paneah is really an Egyptian name. Some suggest that the name Zaphenath-paneah is a Hebrew transcription of an Egyptian name meaning "the god speaks and he lives." Professor Kenneth Kitchen, points out that Zaphenath-paneah was originally *Zat-en-aph*. In ancient Egyptian was pronounced Djed(u)en-ef ('he who is called'). This point, he asserts, is a familiar phrase to all Egyptologists. Furthermore, it is an example of where the letters 't' and 'p,' became reversed. Such orthography illustrates the common (but unintentional) practice whenever difficult words and names are transferred from one language into another. A Hebrew scribe most likely slipped into the use of a common Semitic root *zaphan* while writing zaphenat, for the unfamiliar vocalization of Joseph's Egyptian name. The second part of the name, "Paneah," may be derived from the Egyptian word, "aneah" ankh or ankhu (signifying 'is alive'). The initial "Pa" or "Pi," corresponds to the Egyptian word Ipi or Ipu. Therefore, "Zaphenath pa'aneah" means, "he who is called Anakh." *He who is called Life.* A beautiful way of saying, "Saviour."

[42] Compare with *Matthew 25:35-39*. Is the Lord quoting Joseph?

[43] Remember that in eastern thinking 10 is the number of *witness borne of trial*.

[44] Remember that in eastern thinking 7 is the number of completeness. Joseph was perfect in this thing and therefore received perfection. He credits his physical beauty with living "delicately" and fasting for God's sake. This is fasting not for selfish reasons but to come nearer to God and His will in our lives. We speak in our society of "hard and fast living" and how it takes its toll on the body. Joseph, and Daniel, would agree.

[45] This is just one of many tiny details that prove this book's authenticity. Had this book been a forgery by Middle Age Catholics, it is little details like this that would have exposed it. Nobody in the Middle Ages knew that modern archeologists have connected Memphis with Saqqara (Sakkara), the very center of Imhotep's power and what appears to be the very location from which Joseph sold grain.

[46] Joseph would not have understood this at the time, but she was likely trying to live out an Isis/Horus ritual with him.

[47] Joseph Smith would say something very similar when he gave a sermon on charity. He would say that charity would cover a multitude of sins and that if we had charity in our hearts, much charity would be given to us on the day of judgement. That's a good thing.

⁴⁸ Translations differ here. One refers to this site as *the Hippodrome,* which means "a course for chariot races." This doesn't make sense. Another reads, "Carry ye up the bones of Asenath your mother and lay her beside Rachel my mother who was a descendant of Asef, and bury her there for she is also a descendant of Asef, the same as I am, and all of you are too." It is unclear who Asef was, but we assume it was on Joseph's mother side of the family. This fits with the legend that Asenath was adopted. Rachel was buried in Bethlehem.

⁴⁹ This is Joseph's commission that there would be scripture bearing his tribal name. *See Ezekiel 37:16;19.*

⁵⁰ There are many ancient records which say that Joseph actually became Pharaoh for a season when "his Egyptian father Pharaoh" died and on his deathbed asked Joseph to rule until his young son was able to take the throne. These records say that the famous "Pharaoh who arose who knew not Joseph" was the son of the boy Pharaoh Joseph raised. See *Gospel Feast Vol. 10: Genesis & the Messiah Ben Joseph* for more.

⁵¹ I would argue that at her conversion she was given a new name. I suspect that in a future day we will learn that she was called the *Queen Bee* or *Deseret.* It is possible to read Deseret as meaning (in Eastern Logic anyway) *Zion in the Desert.* In our day Zion in waiting is the City of Israel's Refuge and the Safety of the Messiah Ben Joseph awaiting the Son of God. See *Gospel Feast Series Vol. 10: Genesis & the Messiah Ben Joseph* for more.

⁵² Ancient eastern women suckled their babies from 18 months to 5 years depending on the child. This is saying that Bilhah still had milk (so unless the Lord blessed her with milk just for Benjamin), thus we can deduce that Naphtali was 5 years old or younger at the time. This makes Joseph, Jacob's 10th son instead of his 11th. Eastern thinkers will immediately see why this interests us. 10 is the number of witness born of trial. None of Israel's sons bore more witness in his trails than Joseph.

⁵³ This differs from the common understanding in *Genesis 35:18.* There it is thought that Ben-jamin means "Son at my right hand." This is interesting because where "yamin" does mean hand, "ha-yom" means "the day" or "today." This new understanding is a completely appropriate reading of Ben-ha-yom and one that was not previously known until Benjamin's testimony. If what Jacob meant was Ben Jah-yom that would be even more interesting considering the events surrounding the boy's birth. That would mean "Son of the days of my praise" or "the son we fasted to have." This is a means of celebrating the gift of the boy-child and not burdening him forever with moniker, "I killed my mother." It's little things like this that add weight to the veracity of these testimonies.

⁵⁴ They stripped the Lord of his robe and beat him nude too. In fact, our modern depictions of the crucifixion show Him wearing clothes but that was not how it was done.

[55] People have questioned why the Lord put men like Joseph and Abraham (and Joseph Smith) through some of the things that He did. I think the answer is simpler than many realize. The whole point in our parental gods creating men and women in their own image was to make family. The old adage that it is lonely at the top is far too true. It is one thing to have a cat as a friend but it is entirely another to have a "brother in arms." Men and women who suffer together have joy together. The Lord suffered all things for us. I think some of the tests he put men like Joseph through were to make for Himself, "brothers in arms." Friends who understood what it meant to follow the will of the Father, like He would have to do, over hill and dale. Through the Akidah and Gethsemane. What other purpose would Potiphar's wife and Liberty Jail serve?

[56] This is a brilliant and deep insight into the mind of Lucifer. I once asked a prominent leader of the church a question. I could not understand the mindset of Satan. He said to me, "Reed, Lucifer is schizophrenic, didn't you know that?" I admit that I didn't then, but Benjamin understood it.

[57] The Lord's name in Hebrew is Joshua, which means *Jehovah saves!* So in the original Hebrew this likely reads similar to: "...until the Most High shall send Jesus in the form of His only begotten."

[58] Including a whisper that Joseph and Asenath might have had a daughter too.

[59] Prevailing is the meaning of the word Israel. Joseph prevailed in gaining the birthright just as Jacob did. Joseph, and his clan, have blood right to the name Israel. This is why they took that name for their kingdom when the great spilt happened. You will note that Judah did not fight them over the name. They knew it belonged to Joseph.

[60] compare with *Genesis 48:5–6.*

[61] Sadly it will also be known in part as the and/or the war between Israel & Edom.

[62] The Lord told Joseph Smith that Abraham was ordained a High Priest at the hand of Melchizedek, who was Shem. See *D&C 84:14.*

[63] Muhammed did claim to be a descendant of Ishmael via his first son Nebaioth. Jethro's family, called the Kenites, did marry into the Ishmaelite clans of Arabia.

[64] In Eastern Thinking a covenant is cut and there is some blood that is shed. This was done as a sign of the greatest covenant between God and Man that of the Atonement of Jesus Christ. Between a man and wife, the covenant of their oneness that was cut was her hymen, hence the blood.

[65] see *Exodus 32:10.*

[66] This is a remnant from the empire Alexander the Great set up, just before Rome took over.

67 The Jews should have known this would be trouble since Jehovah told Daniel and Ezekiel that the Jewish nation, would be under the ruling thumb of the Gentiles until the Time of the End. That time was not yet over, so there was no way the people were going to be truly independent.

68 see Joseph Smith article in *The Evening and Morning Star*, March 1834, pg. 143.

69 Christians post 300 A.D. understood this and used it to harm the Jews through the centuries, which is totally unfair. It is crazy to blame modern Jewry for the rejection of Jesus Christ over 2,000 years old. The Lord has a great love for His kindred the Jewish people and has warned the nations that those who mistreat Israel will one day be judged by God accordingly. Joseph Smith further taught that as Latter-day Saints we are to help the Jews fulfill their God given mission as the Lord calls them home to Jerusalem and works to fulfill the promises and destinies promised to them in the Torah and other writings. The Lord chose Judah for great things and those things will all yet come to pass.

70 The hilarious thing is that today these same Luciferians believe in a fantasy paradigm where they can in Star Trek like fashion know the future through Science Fiction Technology or by Remote Viewing or by Familiar Spirits. It's okay for them to believe in hocus pocus but if you believe in Biblical prophecy, you are called the nut. Well, bibbidi bobbidi boo hoo!

71 The prime example is the Donation of Constantine, see *Vol. 1: Daniel & the Last Days*.

72 I am convinced that this is the message behind our latter-day call to keep a journal. We have been promised by our prophets that keeping a journal, or at least leaving behind some sort of spiritual testimony, will be a source of strength for our children. I believe we all can witness that we have taken courage and strength from the personal story and testimony of those of our ancestors who have done this.

73 There are always some minor variations by translator when moving a text from one language to another. It is impossible (without a Urim & Thummim) to translate 100% precisely due to cultural understandings (hence our push to think more eastern).

74 Ginzberg says: "Job, or, as he is sometimes called, Jobab, was, indeed, king of Edom, the land wherein wicked plans are concocted against God, wherefore it is called also Uz, [meaning] "counsel."

75 Ginzberg says that their fathers were, Shuah, Naamat, and Barachel, respectively. These were the sons of Buz, who was a brother of Job and a nephew of Abraham. This would make Bildad, Zophar, and Elihu cousins. Exactly how Buz could be a nephew of Abraham when Job was great grand son is not clear but with the inter-marrying going on in Abraham's family, and the incest in Esau's family, combined with the differing longevity of the global family, it is entirely possible. When in doubt sing "I'm My Own Grandpa."